WHAT THE HELL JUST HAPPENED?

Acknowledgements

Wow, what a journey! Only a couple of months ago, before writing the first words of this book, What The Hell Just Happened? I was sceptical about sharing our story. Would people judge us? Would it sound too dramatic? Would it destroy me? The answer is the opposite.

Jules came up with the idea of writing this book to help others who may be on a journey of adversity. Having written a book on football and then a fun self-help book for teens, this one was going to be difficult.

That was when we were introduced to fellow author and soul writer, Cassandra Farren, who has been an immense source of help and inspiration. Cassie has guided us through this process every step of the way (and even gave us a packet of tissues in preparation for the tears).

Pouring out our feelings onto paper brought us many tears and there have been a number of comforting hugs during this process. Thank you, Cassie, for helping us to share our story and find peace in adversity.

Thanks to our wonderful family, but especially to Daniel, Russell, Louise, Warwick and Roxanne for their unwavering support and love. It meant the world to us. To Mum and Nan for understanding the effects this had on their little boy.

To our friends who have listened when we've needed a chat, a hug or to make us laugh when we've needed it. The wonderful people we've met at Isebrook Hospital in the support groups and the charity that Jules is now a big part of, Breast Friends Northamptonshire.

More thanks go to Michael Wright and Melissa James of Millennial Creative for designing the cover and to John Cox for typesetting the script. To Gemma Stephens and Hazel Napier for being our proof-readers.

Love Mark and Jules

First published in 2020 in the UK

Welford Publishing

A catalogue number for this book is available from the British Library - ISBN 978-1-916267-12-1

Cover design and illustrations Millennial Creative
www.millennialcreative.co.uk

Disclaimer
This book is designed to provide helpful information on the subjects discussed. It is general reference information and should not be used to diagnose any medical problem and is not intended as a substitute for consulting with a medical or professional practitioner.

Dedication

From Mark

For my wonderful wife Jules, my inspiration and my best friend. Thank you for being there through the tough times my damaged brain gave us. Thank you to our lovely family and everyone else who picked us both up when we needed it x

From Jules

For my Dad, my rock and the best a girl could ever have wanted and needed. I wish you'd had the time to put your memoirs down as you wanted. You were the most exceptionally, exciting, inspiring and caring person that made everyone who knew you, listen to your every word. I love and miss you and hope I've made you as proud of me as I am of you x

About the Authors

Mark and Jules are from Northampton, England and are described as "a great couple who are always smiling." Met at work and then married in 2003, they share a passion for helping individuals change their lives.

They run two part time businesses. The first is in a network marketing company where they help people save money and work towards a better financial future. The other is their own business, established in 2009 and called the Future Toolbox, which teaches life skills for teenagers and young adults that the education system doesn't. Mark and Jules were proud to win the Best Enterprising Business Award in 2018 and 2019 for Northamptonshire and had their last book shortlisted for the finals of a writer's award.

Their passions are travelling the world: having been on many trips to some amazing places, from a week on the beach to a city break to a backpacking adventure, it is their desire to enjoy experiencing real cultures. Health and fitness are important as is eating lovely healthy food and watching our incredible family develop.

Contact us

Website: www.kennedyauthors.co.uk
Email: mail@mad4life.co.uk

And follow us:
@kennedyauthors - Instagram - Twitter - Facebook

Introduction

Jules:
At the time of writing this I am 56 years old, I have two wonderful grown up sons and four amazing grandchildren whom I love dearly.

I spent a great deal of time as a single parent until 18 years ago meeting my adorable husband Mark. As you read through this story we had what can almost be described as the perfect marriage until a series of unfortunate events led us down a path neither of us expected, wanted or knew how to deal with.

I decided one evening after going to bed that I felt it was time to share my story, not because I wanted anyone to feel sorry for me, but because I knew there must be hundreds of partners in the world going through what I did and not knowing what was happening nor where or how to get help. I wanted them to read this and not to endure the years of heartbreak and uncertainty I did.

After gaining Mark's permission to write our story, as it would contain lots of personal details about him, he decided he would like to help write the book but from his perspective too. So you will see as you start reading, it is unique, as each chapter begins with my story and followed by Mark's version.

I hope you enjoy reading this and understand way before we did how mental health can manifest itself even in the strongest of people and take over your lives. We now know that it is ok not to be ok and we have found our coping mechanisms and hope that by reading this you too can find peace within mental health.

Mark:

As Jules says, we had an easy going and relaxed lifestyle up until 2012 when life threw us a few challenges (to say the least). Sometimes things happen that are beyond your control and the key is how you deal with them. Being a positive couple, we sort of decided to try and carry on with life as it was before but that is easier said than done.

At first I was very sceptical and nervous about sharing our story (and I still am) but we want to help other to realise that there is a way to overcome adversity. Also, writing has been extremely cathartic as it has helped me to unload a lot of trauma that I've suffered following my injury (read more about that later).

Please read on and come on our journey with us. If we can give you even the smallest of takeaways to help you on your journey, then our goal of writing this book has been achieved.

Chapter 1: Jules

January 2019

What the hell just happened? I'm in shock, sobbing my heart out whilst wrapped up in a throw on our sofa. It's 11pm I should be cuddled up in bed next to my husband, but instead he's sat next to me throwing question after question at me. I feel totally broken that our life has been ripped apart at the seams. Surely this can't be happening? Not to me, not to us! My tears continue to fall as I try to process the words that have shattered my soul. My husband, Mark, told me half an hour earlier that he no longer wants to carry on with our marriage! How can he say that, how can he feel that this is possibly the end? I've done everything I can to understand what he's been through. I have tried my hardest to support him and be patient with the never-ending mood swings, the silences, the confusion, the frustrations, the crying, the anxiety and depression and oh not to mention the endless sleepless nights. Is this really the end of our life together?

Tonight was the final straw, I can't take any more and I just want to be left alone. He eventually goes back to bed and I'm left wondering how, or if, I can pick my life up yet again and where would I begin? Am I strong enough to do this?

Hang on, maybe he's right? Maybe this is the right decision? Do I really want this life of uncertainty, pain, doubt, self-loathing, selfishness and constantly feeling scared of our whole existence falling apart? I'm 56 years old now, I'd always hoped that by this time in my life things would be easier; I had a beautiful vision of being happy and carefree. Instead I'm living with a stranger (aka my husband) who is so eaten by anxiety and depression through the day, that he spends most nights hugging the toilet being sick or lying next to me crying himself to sleep. He's a complete shell of the person he used to be, he loathes himself and his behaviour and we're just stuck together in this hopeless abyss of pain and total sadness.

But no, NO! I don't want this. This is NOT what I want. I want my old life back, the life we had when everything was simple. I want my husband back, the one I married, the one without the dark depressions, the one without the total self-doubt, the one with the confidence and belief that he could do and achieve anything he wanted. The husband I could say anything to without any recourse, the husband who could talk to me and tell me how he was feeling. I feel so alone with this now as I lay trembling and crying. How can I possibly tell my children what has just happened? How are they going react? They have been my rock the past few years.

Up until *the incident* that turned our lives upside down, we had what can really only be described as the perfect marriage (yes, really!). We'd fallen head over heels in love and both had virtually the same interests of football, fitness, socialising with friends or just spending quality time together, travelling, going on holidays, listening to music and going to see bands we loved. We did what we wanted, when we wanted and we both loved life. Mark and I both had good jobs, then we started up our own business as motivational speakers in schools which was a dream we'd always had. The business was going really well, and Mark was freelancing with a company that gave us bookings within schools up and down the country whilst I kept on my job working for a national organisation running a training centre here in Northampton. My children were all grown up by this time so if we fancied doing something, we literally would just do it without having any other commitments to worry about. Seriously, life was a breeze with so much fun, laughter and most of all so much love.

We first met when we were working at a post 16 education company delivering apprenticeships and finding employment for school leavers. When I first met Mark to be honest, he didn't blow me away. I actually thought he was just a 'bit of a lad', nice enough but the earth certainly didn't move for me. Gradually though as we got to know each other I realised what a really great person he was and I thought, wouldn't it be good to get to know him even better? Little did I know that he was thinking the same about me! Then came the fateful Christmas do; the kiss on the dance floor and the rest, as they say, is history. We were married on the 1st August 2003 and were blissfully happy. That was until we went on a fateful holiday in August 2012 to Fuerteventura.

Chapter 2: Mark

What the hell just happened? Have you ever had a moment when you're wide awake, but it feels like you're stuck in the middle of a horrific nightmare? Why is Jules crying on the sofa when she should be cuddled up in bed next to me?

It broke my heart to see her this way, but I didn't know what to say or do to make it better. All I knew was that I didn't want to lose the woman I loved. I couldn't bear the thought of not having Jules in my life, she's everything I'd ever wanted and so much more. We were great together, everyone said so. What have I done? She said I've broken her, but I just don't understand. It's too much to take in. How did I break up this amazing life that we had together? How have I caused so much hurt to the most wonderful person in my life? Is time travel possible? I wish I could turn back time.

Have you ever found out that something's happened to you, but you can't remember what it was? Well this was one of those moments! I'm not talking about one of those '*had a few drinks and blacked out*' moments. I'm talking about a moment where you're completely stone cold sober, but you genuinely have no recollection of an event. If it had never happened to me, I may find it harder to believe, but believe me when I say it's real. This was one of those moments when I felt so confused and frustrated, why couldn't I remember what had happened?

I headed back upstairs to bed, glancing over my shoulder and seeing Jules still on the sofa, wrapped in a throw. It was dark and I knew she was upset. Everything was a total blur from then on as I got into bed and drifted in and out of consciousness. It's not the same as sleep, it's like a sort of coma, being in another world where a dream state seems real.

One minute I'm on stage and delivering a speech but then the words don't come out of my mouth. People start walking out of the room and things are going badly. Then suddenly, boom! I'm awake.

The room is dark, life is real. Panic sets in! I'm alone! I'm hurting and broken! And then as soon as I wake, I'm unconscious again. This happens again and again until the world becomes real.

It's 8:30am and the sun is shining. My head hurts. It feels as if I've been hit on the right side, just above my ear. After searching the house, I realise that Jules isn't home. I think I heard the front door shut earlier but that could've been part of that dreamlike foggy state. Nope it was real, Jules had left. I remembered that she had an appointment to get her nails done. It's just a nail appointment, I tell myself. She will come back, won't she?

Sitting in the conservatory, reality starts to set in. I've broken it again but is it repairable? How can I do this to the love of my life? What have I done to the love of my life? The problem is I genuinely can't remember. Jules says that I say things that I have no recollection of, and she's even said I've lied about things, but I just can't remember, am I lying? I'm starting to question my life and I'm starting to question myself.

My head still hurts! It's not a headache, it's a dull ache. It's heavy, my brain is heavy! Then panic sets in. I can't breathe and I want to scream. Have you seen that moment in a scary film where the victim is completely frozen in front of the zombie? They want to run but can't, so they stay in the moment of panic before the zombie eats them? I'm that victim and that zombie is just about to consume me. I want to cry but nothing will come out. I want to scream but my voice is silent. I want to hug my wife but she's not here.

The next part is a blur. It could be minutes, or it could be hours. Conscious thoughts of how horrible I am. How can I repair what I've broken? How can I get my wife to love me again? How can I shake this anxiety, this panic, this pain and this hurt? Is life really this horrible now? What type of awful person have I become?

Then reason kicks in. Of course I can fix it. Our love is stronger than anything I have known. We've been married for 16 years and I genuinely cannot imagine my life without Jules in it. That's not going to happen. We can get through this, right? Surely we can. It's not my fault and it's not Jules's fault. What's happened has happened and we can get past this. We will get past this.

I need to see her now and tell her how sorry I am. I'll get help, I'll do what I can to fix it. Time travel isn't possible but the future is. Move forward not backwards, right? Trouble is, I don't know what's happened. Brain wracking, thoughts whirring, head hurting...what the hell happened? I think I've done something really bad, but I don't know what it is.

You could say that our life before *the incident* was pretty carefree. It was spontaneous, fun, exciting and laid back. I considered myself to be a very lucky man. Meeting and marrying Jules when I was in my late 20s was the best thing that ever happened to me. We had an amazing life together right from the beginning, I loved and accepted her boys as my own and we lived our life to the full. If we fancied doing something, then we generally did it. From holidays to football matches to weekends away to music gigs and crazy nights out. In fact, I was usually described as the ultimate laid-back bloke. People used to ask if anything stressed me out and, to be honest, very little did. My only real downside was when my football team, Northampton Town, lost. Jules and I just smiled, laughed and had endless pots of energy. If we thought something seemed a good idea, then we generally went ahead with it.

In 2009, I made the move to become my own boss and a year later, I was made redundant from my job of 14 years. It was time to seize the moment and throw everything into a new venture. It was so exciting freelancing, travelling around the country and delivering motivation sessions to teenagers in schools. Getting up early and driving to Lancashire or Kent was something I would never have considered before, but I was thriving and learning new things along the way. Jules continued her job as training manager, running a successful training centre.

We loved our holidays together and in August 2012, we booked a last-minute week away in Fuerteventura. We'd been to the island a couple of times and had an amazing time and this time we opted to stay in the south of the island instead of in the north. We couldn't wait to explore, visit our favourite beaches and create some new amazing memories. Well, that was the plan...

It was that wonderful summer when England was alive with the excitement of the Olympics. We'd been down to London and attended a couple of the events, catching the buzz of everything.

Do you remember *'Super Saturday'* when Mo Farah won the 10,000 metres, Jess Ennis clinched the Heptathlon gold and Greg Rutherford won the long jump? We were jumping around our living room like crazy people celebrating our GB athletes winning in London.

Well, one week later we were standing in the reception of the Althay Apartments Hotel in Fuerteventura watching Mo make history winning the 5,000 metre gold. The hotel had a small, old TV perched on the ledge of the check-in desk. We had to ask the receptionist to find the channel for us and yes, he thought we were mad! When Mo crossed the line, we celebrated with a couple of other English guests and finished our drinks. We were in good spirits and decided to head out to a little tapas bar around the corner from the hotel, surely the food there had to be better than the all-inclusive buffet on offer?

We sat at our table chatting and looking forward to the evening ahead; it was quiet and there was another couple eating near us. The starter of octopus arrived, and we began eating. My last memory of that evening was getting up to go to the toilet. The next question begged is, what the hell happened?

Chapter 3: Jules

I was sitting in the restaurant when I suddenly became aware that the waiters were looking at me strangely with our main meals. It then dawned on me that Mark had been gone for some time. Bet he's gotten talking to someone, I thought, so off I went to locate him. On finding the gents toilet, I knocked on the door. He opened it and what I saw completely shocked me to the core.

"What's happened?" I asked.

Mark didn't resemble the same man who had walked into the toilets. His skin was almost a grey colour, he was sweating, his eyes were all over the place and he was unable to focus!

"I don't know" he said, "but I feel really weird."

I managed to get him to come and sit back at our table. Thankfully the restaurant wasn't full and there was only one other couple dining there.

The waiter came and asked if everything was alright to which I replied, "I'm not sure."

It was at that point blood just came pouring out of Mark's nose at an alarming rate. He started to panic somewhat at seeing this blood as I was frantically trying to find a napkin.

"Please help me!" I yelled to the waiter. The couple behind who were clearly Spanish and didn't speak great English nor I great Spanish (ordering beer and food was as much as I could do) began panicking and asking what was going on. I really didn't have a clue as to why this was happening and became very fearful.

"Please get me a doctor, I need a doctor now!" I kept repeating to anyone that would listen.

Mark then said he felt really sick, so I got him out onto the roadside where he started violently vomiting. The waiter came along and said they'd called for an ambulance and it was on its way.

I couldn't say how long that took as I was just focused on looking after Mark and trying to make head or tail in my mind on what the hell was going on! I kept mopping up the blood from his nose and at this point he wasn't really saying anything.

The ambulance turned up and they put him in a wheelchair, then started asking me questions to which I had no answer. It was extremely difficult as their English was as poor as my Spanish. However, they asked him his name to which he replied *'Mark'*. They asked him where he was from and he couldn't remember. I told him we're in Fuerteventura and he replied, *'Why are we here? When did we get here?'*

I tried replying sensibly that we're on holiday and arrived the day before, but he just couldn't grasp where we were. They asked him some more questions like *'Do you know what day it is? How old are you? When were you born?'* He had no idea whatsoever and was now becoming distressed and very confused.

The paramedics said he needed to go to the hospital and started pushing the wheelchair into the back of the ambulance. I went to go in with him but they refused to let me. I grew very upset as I could see how confused and agitated he was. I wanted to be with him to help calm him but they flatly refused and made me sit in the front with the driver. To be honest I have very little recollection of the drive as my mind was trying to make sense of what the hell had just happened. I couldn't process it; one minute we were having a lovely evening, the food we had eaten was delicious, we were chatting and having fun and then he just went to the toilet. That was it; that was all I knew. I kept trying to think what the fuck actually happened?

On arrival at the hospital we were taken to the A&E department and asked if I had *'papers'* which I said *'yes'* guessing they meant insurance and they left us in a cubicle. Mark by this time was, for all intents and purposes, unconscious but anytime he did come around he was freaking out at the blood on his hands and wondering where he was. I managed to find some tissues and washed the blood off him to stop him panicking when he saw it. A lady doctor and a nurse then came to see us and asked what had happened. Again, the language barrier caused some issues, but they did a slight examination of him. I explained that the last time he woke he complained of a pain in his ear. They asked me if he had any alcohol that day. I replied, '*Yes we've had four drinks.*' I wanted to make sure they knew, in case they needed to give him anything, that he did have alcohol in his system.

The doctor then took a look inside his ear and stated he has an ear infection. This wasn't an uncommon thing as he used to suffer with these, so I just kind of accepted it. They then came back and gave him an injection in his bum, gave me a prescription for the said infection and told me to go back to our hotel and that he was just *'drunk!'* Drunk? They honestly thought this was self-inflicted through alcohol? This made me really angry and upset. I could see by her face she was thinking we were typical Brits abroad who can't handle their drink. We weren't drunk, we'd had a few drinks and we certainly aren't the people that go out and get completely drunk every night on holiday. How bloody dare she! They asked if I had money, which I did, then ordered us a taxi. That was it, that was all they did but, in all honesty, I couldn't give them any further ideas as to what had happened as I didn't know myself.

The taxi journey back seemed to take forever. Mark was laid out on the back-seat unconscious or asleep and I was in the front. I did panic a little as I thought the male driver really could take us anywhere. I didn't know whereabouts we were on the island or how to get back to our hotel. He did get us back safely thankfully.

I managed to rouse Mark to get him out of the taxi, but he was struggling to stay awake and couldn't walk properly. I had to hold him up and help him put one foot in front of the other. He was still extremely confused and distressed. The hotel security guard took one look at him and started tut-tutting and shaking his head assuming Mark was totally inebriated; oh my god, if I hadn't been holding Mark up, I swear I would have punched his lights out at that moment!

By trying to convince Mark that we were actually at our home, I calmed him down a little. I got him to walk the short way through the hotel and up the steps into our apartment and to lay down on our bed. He fell into a deep sleep and I spent the rest of the night sitting next to him on the bed watching him, scared to death of what might happen to him and also trying with all my might to piece together what the hell just happened!

Whilst watching Mark sleep I noticed a graze and a bruise forming on his right shoulder. It got me thinking, maybe he slipped over and hit his head? I had no answers to the endless questions and I'd never felt so scared in my entire life. He's going to be OK, isn't he? He has to be OK.

After what felt like an eternity, Mark awoke, looked at me with his lovely smile and tried to move but it clearly hurt him. He asked, "Did we have a lot to drink last night, my head really hurts and feels so heavy?"

I replied, "No, we didn't drink much, do you remember anything about what happened last night?"

Chapter 4: Mark

Jules was sitting on the edge of the bed staring at me as I slowly opened my eyes. I asked her if we had gotten drunk last night as I tried to sit up. I was in a lot of pain and by the look on her face immediately sensed there was something seriously wrong,

After hearing Jules's account of the previous night's events: going to the toilet, nosebleeds, being violently sick, going to hospital and then taking over an hour to get from the taxi to the room before passing out, I was stunned. I would've thought she was making it all up had it not been for her very serious face and my very sore head. It didn't make sense.

Suddenly I became aware of my surroundings; the sun was shining into the room of our hotel, we were in Costa Calma in Fuerteventura. I tried to replay my memories from the night before; Mo Farah won the Olympic 5,000 metres; we went to a tapas bar and then...blank! Nothing. Absolutely nothing!

You may be reading this and wondering if I'd overdone it with the celebratory beers, but I can tell you now, I'd only had a few and what I was experiencing was nothing like a hangover. How could I not remember a whole evening from my life and now be in so much pain? I could tell Jules was concerned but my head couldn't function despite trying so hard to try and make sense of what had happened.

I spent the whole of that Sunday in a blur, basically sleeping and throwing up. Monday came around and I managed to get out of bed and lay on the sofa bed in the living room of the apartment. Jules continued her regular checks on me as I drifted between sleeping, drinking water and having conversations trying to work out what the hell had happened. The hospital had discharged me with an ear infection and prescribed antibiotics, which contained penicillin, so that explained the sickness. I'm allergic to penicillin. Thankfully the throwing up stopped when I stopped taking the pills.

Tuesday arrived, I woke up and said, "Right, I can't stay in the room any longer!"

Jules wanted to call a doctor because, naturally, she was getting more and more worried. The pain in my head was still there and I still wasn't right. I got dressed and we called a taxi to make a trip to the local doctor. The receptionist looked a little confused when we asked for a taxi and we then learned that it was only a two-minute drive; in fact the meter was still on one Euro when we arrived.

After a quick examination, the doctor confirmed I had blood in my ear and asked me to return on Thursday to see if I would be allowed to fly home. Faced with the choice of another day in a hotel room, we decided to go for a little walk and then back to sit by the pool. I even managed to eat some food that evening for the first time.

Wednesday, I did what most blokes do, I insisted that I was fine and drove us to the beach. It was liberating to be outside, away from that dreaded hotel and being able to eat some proper food surrounded by surfers and sun bathers.

Thursday was great news; I could fly home the following day so what better way to celebrate than another drive to the beach. Although I felt groggy, I knew the worry and angst that Jules was going through, so I just brushed everything aside.

We went home on Friday and I felt scared. Sitting on a bench on the sea front, reality suddenly kicked in. This is serious! I have a head injury! What happens if my head explodes on the plane just after take-off? No joke, if I pass out or have a seizure, the plane would have to make an emergency landing. What if were mid-flight and I collapse? What's gonna happen when we get home and I go to A&E? What the hell happened last Saturday? How am I going to explain this to everyone?

The flight was awful! Firstly, it was full, and we were crammed in a space by the window near the front. Fine, no worries. Then the lady in front decided to recline her seat just as I put my bag underneath my seat. BANG! It caught the right side of my head and I said something a little more than, '*oh bother!*' Anyway, we made it, landed at Stansted, got through passport control, Jules drove home and we got to bed in the early hours.

The next day was indescribable! I woke in our bed on the hottest day of the year. Jules had already spoken to Northampton General Hospital and we were advised to go for an X-ray at A&E. It's a 15-minute walk so off we headed. There was lots of waiting, chatting, blood pressure taking, more chatting, more questions before a CT scan and then a bit more waiting.

Russell (Jules's son) and Roxanne (our future daughter-in-law) arrived home from holiday that day too and their lift had let them down at the last minute. I told Jules to go and pick them up from Luton whilst I waited for the results of my scan to come back and then I'd walk home. No big deal, I'd walked there after all.

An hour later, a nurse came to see me on the ward where I was waiting and informed me that I was to go immediately to John Radcliffe Hospital in Oxford as they weren't happy with the results of the scan. It was confirmed I'd fractured my skull but there was something they wanted '*to check*'. I took this news in my stride, thinking it was better to be safe than sorry and at this point, I called Jules and told her the plan and to come and pick me up from Oxford.

The ambulance journey was sort of fun. Yes, it's weird in a crisis situation in your life that you can refer to something as *fun*, but that's always been my character, to look on the bright side. The driver was retiring that day and I was his last drive and the lady paramedic was absolutely lovely. We chatted all the way there and she reassured me that everything was going to be fine. Even though the ambulance had its blue lights flashing, I somehow still hadn't grasped the seriousness of the situation.

They dropped me at John Radcliffe and I was taken into a private room where I waited for Jules to arrive. Suddenly I realised that this may be a little more serious than expected. The friendly ambulance guys had been replaced by some quite serious-looking medics and the view from my window overlooked the air ambulance heli-pad with the bird taking off and landing at intervals.

More blood pressure checks, chats, waiting, more chats and then just as Jules arrived with Russell, Roxanne and Daniel (Jules's other son), we were summoned by a doctor into a separate room. I will never forget his words.

"You're lucky to survive, people don't usually wake up after this trauma to the brain. We need to operate immediately!"

We almost fell off our chairs as the doc showed us the scan. There was a huge mass on the right side of my head and a smaller one on the left. I'd fallen on my right side and the impact to my head was so intense that it had shifted my brain, causing it to hit the left side!

Words like seizure, epilepsy, fit, death and major operation dominated the next few minutes but it was all a blur. We suddenly learned what a subdural haematoma, a burr hole procedure and a craniotomy meant very quickly. In short, number one is a blood clot; I had two of them! The huge masses on the scan showed one of 6cm (right) and the other of 2cm (left). Point two is where they drill into your brain to disperse the subdural haematoma, but I couldn't have one of those because the clot was too big, so the next suggestion was number three.

Oh my life! Number three was unimaginable! I still shiver and feel sick inside when I read the definition of this!

During a craniotomy, the neurosurgeon will remove a section of bone to create access, then remove the blood clot. When the procedure is complete, the surgeon will replace the section of bone and close up the soft tissue using sutures or staples. The recovery involves between three to six months in hospital and that's before the skull is reattached!

Three to six months? I couldn't tell you the last time I had three to six *days* off work! The thought of any of the operations was unimaginable. My head was spinning as I looked around at the sea of shocked faces that surrounded me. Was this really happening? Were they talking about *my* brain? I was walking, talking and functioning just fine; surely, they can't be serious about asking me to agree to a potentially life-threatening operation?

All of a sudden, it was like a force of strength came over me as these words came out of my mouth before I could stop them.

"No, I don't think I need that," I confidently told the doctor, "I feel fine and I know I can survive!"

Jules looked at me with tears in her eyes. What the hell just happened there? I've just been told that people don't survive this brain injury and I'm feeling inside that I've done the hard bit. I knew that I was going to be fine. The doctor reluctantly agreed to give me the night to think about it and he would see me again in the morning. I went away for a relaxing holiday and came back needing a potentially life-threatening operation, surely this can't be happening?

Chapter 5: Jules

It turned out that Mark had absolutely no recollection other than watching the Olympics and going to the restaurant. Then no memory of the events afterwards whatsoever.

After explaining what happened I could see he was quite shaken and managed to get up and go to the bathroom. He was still feeling very woozy and struggling to focus and see properly. He also kept spitting blood which was concerning him. We tried to piece together what may have happened due to the bruise on his right shoulder, but didn't really get very far. We agreed for him to rest and I would go and get the prescription. That was a big mistake! I got it ok after eventually finding a pharmacy and he took the tablets, but then was violently sick again. It turned out that they were penicillin and Mark's allergic to penicillin!

I wanted to fetch a doctor, but Mark felt that after a good night's rest, all would be fine. He slept all day. Monday morning came and he tried to get up but could only make it to the living room and slept on the sofa. I did manage to get a little food inside him throughout the day but he wasn't improving. I'm getting more and more anxious about his wellbeing and just really wanted to get him to a doctor and to get him home.

Tuesday morning came and there had still been no improvement. I had barely slept and felt physically and emotionally drained. Mark was a fit and healthy 38-year-old man, why wasn't he getting any better? We needed some help, and this time I wasn't going to be fobbed off with being told that my husband was drunk! I suspected Mark wouldn't be keen but I'd had enough of the constant worry.

"That's it! I'm getting you to the doctor, we need help. I feel really scared that something terrible has happened." Mark didn't object this time; I think he wanted some answers too.

We managed to get to hotel reception who called us a taxi and we got in.

"Can you take us to the nearest doctors please?" I asked the driver. He looked quite bemused and repeated,

"Doctor?"

"Yes", I said quite sternly and off we went. It actually turned out that the surgery was only around the next corner, no wonder he'd looked at me quizzically!

The doctor we saw was quite good, he listened to our story and examined Mark. On looking into his right ear, he said, "There's a lot of blood and swelling in there, when do you fly home?"

"Friday!" I replied, and he said he couldn't at that point allow Mark to fly.

I'm beside myself now, what is wrong with Mark? Why is there so much blood in his ear? How and where are we going to stay? What about our work commitments? All these things and more were going around in my head and just real panic about what to do next. The doctor recommended rest and for us to come and see him again on the Thursday for another assessment. That was it, what on earth do we do now, what if we can't get home, what are they going to do to help Mark?

We went back to the hotel and I found a nice sunbed by the pool in the shade for Mark and well, we just rested. At this point in time we had a mobile phone with us but it wasn't one we could use abroad. It was well before the real uptake on Wi-Fi etc. so the only contact I had with my family back home was by using an old pc in the lobby in which I had to put a Euro for an hour's use. Sending messages through Facebook wasn't an ideal way to let our close family know what had happened, but we didn't have much choice. I did keep it brief so as not to worry them too much although I felt so incredibly alone and scared.

We went back to the doctors on Thursday; we walked this time though! He examined Mark again and although the blood and swelling was still there, Mark had improved in terms of his focus and alertness so he agreed that we could fly home the next day, Friday, and gave us some strong ibuprofen to take half an hour before the flight. Yes, finally, we're going home! I'm so very relieved but still terrified of how Mark would cope with the flight. I was petrified something may go wrong and we'd be stuck 37,000 feet in mid-air! It felt strange arriving at the airport that evening and being desperate to get on our flight and get home. Normally we'd be joking to each other about staying for another week! Not this time; I didn't want to stay for another minute.

Apart from the person in front of Mark on the plane, pushing their seat back just as he was leaning forward to get something out of his bag and banging into his head, the flight went smoothly and we got home around midnight. Mark went straight to bed, but I slept intermittently as I couldn't wait for the morning to ring the local hospital.

It took quite some time for him to be seen the next morning but eventually a great doctor listened to our story and I made sure he looked into Mark's ear. He immediately arranged for a brain scan and Mark was then put onto a ward whilst awaiting the results. He was quite confused as to why they had done this as he kept saying,

"Why are they keeping me in? I feel fine, this is silly."

On this day our son, Russell, was flying back from, (yes can you believe it?), Fuerteventura in very high spirits as he'd left England with his girlfriend, Roxanne, and was returning home, after proposing, with his fiancée! They messaged to say their arranged lift had cancelled and could I pick them up. I tried to get someone else to but they were busy so we agreed I'd go and fetch them home. They were aware of what had happened, but we'd struggled with communications. Although I'd written down Roxanne's mobile number and tried numerous times to call her from a phone box, I'd missed a digit off by mistake, just to add to the difficulties hey! Mark was still joking about feeling fine and wondering why he was on the ward.

I'd just gotten to the airport when Mark phoned to say '*don't worry*', so immediately I panicked and wanted to know what had happened.

"I'm in an ambulance with the blue lights on being taken to John Radcliffe Hospital in Oxford. The hospital sent the results of the scan over to them and they want to see me straight away."

He tried his best to convince me everything was OK and he was feeling great. I felt dreadful and wished I hadn't left him but what could I do? I just expected that he would be home when I got back with reassurances that all was going to be fine. I was worried as to how he was coping, he still was keeping up appearances and trying to make light of it all, but I know now things were going to get a whole lot worse.

Russell and Roxanne arrived and gave me a hug and I just burst into tears and held them so tightly. Boy did I need that at that moment. I drove back home to Northampton, picked up our other son, Daniel, and headed to John Radcliffe to see Mark. That journey seemed to take forever and whilst we were all hugely excited that Russell and Roxanne were to be married, there were long silences as we all tried to process the events that had happened and what we were going to find out. Nothing could have prepared us for what we were about to learn.

We got to Mark's room in the hospital just as a consultant was calling him through to his office. I went with him and they asked us what had happened and then showed us the results of the scan. Oh my god, I couldn't believe what I was seeing, nor what the consultant was telling us.

As we'd imagined, Mark had '*banged*' his head, but it was with such a force that he had a 6cm bleed to his right side of his brain (hence the blood in his ear). He'd hit his head so hard he had actually managed to move his brain which had caused another bleed on the left side! He'd fractured his skull and broken bones in his right ear. So much for the initial diagnosis of an '*ear infection*' from the doctor in Fuerteventura A&E!!!

I felt sick, we were both in shock. The screen we were looking at showed Mark's brain. We just couldn't take it in. The consultant told us they'd not seen many people survive such a traumatic brain injury, just half of the damage he had sustained was enough to kill most people. How on earth was he still alive let alone sitting here talking coherently?

The consultant was adamant Mark needed immediate brain surgery to drain the bleeds because, if they moved and touched his brain, apparently that would be it, he would die! It was too much to take in. We're both trembling, tearful and scared beyond belief, how could this have happened and how did he manage to survive this?

After lengthy discussions with our consultant and another who had come to join the party, we looked at the pros and cons of surgery, which we were incredibly scared of either way. If we didn't go ahead the risk was huge that the bleeds would move and touch his brain. However, the risks of full brain surgery almost had the same outcomes. Eventually as Mark seemed very agitated about the (horrifying!) idea of having his skull opened up they agreed to give us until the morning to talk it through with our family. We knew they needed a decision quickly, but they knew Mark had already managed to '*survive*' seven days with these horrific life-threatening injuries.

The next hour was a bit of a blur, explaining what we'd just been told to the kids. The consultant came into our room and went over all the details again. It was getting late, so we had to leave Mark at the hospital. It was so distressing, I could see he was scared and fearful but Mark, being positive Mark, put on a brave face for us. The thought of him being there all on his own with no-one to talk to or hold broke my heart. I didn't want to go home but what else could I do?

I went to bed feeling completely exhausted, but no matter how hard I tried, I couldn't sleep as the endless questions began to spin around my mind. Is he going to die? Will he have fits now? Should he have the operation? And how on earth has he survived this long?

I got up at about 3am as I needed some tea and Russell, who was staying over, followed me down as he couldn't sleep either. So, there we sat on our kitchen step contemplating what the future may hold and just hugging each other. I tried to go back to sleep but by 5am I thought, fuck it. I got dressed and drove all the way back to John Radcliffe. The security there is really tight around the wards but somehow, I managed to get into the hospital and into Mark's room. He was a little surprised to see me so early, but I could see the joy and relief on his face when he beamed me the biggest smile. I climbed onto his bed where we just lay holding each other and both fell asleep for a short while. He hadn't been able to sleep either, with loads of questions going through his mind. It was no wonder as he was also fearful of what the future would hold for him.

Mark kept saying since we'd gotten back from Fuerteventura that he felt ok and he kept saying it again that morning. "I feel ok Jules, I'm sure I can get through this without the operation."

In all honesty the operation terrified the life out of him, but I had seen first-hand how he'd coped and improved over the past eight days and I felt I needed to trust his instincts and of course, his wishes. So, we told the doctors of our decision not to have surgery and hoped that the bleeds would disperse naturally, and all would be fine. It's fair to say they were a little shocked, but they respected our decision.

We left with an appointment to come back the following week, and that was it. We were just categorically told that Mark mustn't be left alone in case he does fit or anything untoward starts happening. Thank god Russell and Roxanne were staying at ours for the few weeks, as she's a fully qualified nurse and he's a trained Army medic. At least I could leave him if I needed to, knowing he was in safe hands!

Nobody realised that Mark's next appointment date was actually on a bank holiday, so it had to be changed; it was actually almost three weeks before we got seen again. They scanned Mark and the results showed the bleeds were still there, but his brain was now back in its rightful position. Woohoo! Thank goodness for that, things were moving in the right direction.

The hospital didn't want to see him again for another four weeks which took us to mid-October. We asked what we needed to do and what activities Mark could do etc. He's a keen football follower and player of a local fans team, but he was told absolutely no contact sport or any activity that may result in any kind of knock to his head. Although Mark did ask if he was allowed a pint of beer. The consultant said yes but don't go mad! We asked if Mark can still work and whether he can go out for a run. We were just told everything in moderation and for Mark to listen to his body; a gentle small jog maybe to begin with and see how he feels. We asked if there was anything else we needed to know or look out for. He said to avoid long periods of looking at screens (i.e. laptop, TV, mobile) or reading. Take lots of rest and just go and carry on as normal. So off we went really pleased with that and the fact his brain was back where it should be, progression, yay! There were no leaflets on brain injury to read, no websites to research and no recommendation of support groups to join. We didn't think to ask about any further support; as far as we were concerned, Mark needed to take it easy but in time, our life would return to normal.

Little did we know what was going to happen next.

Chapter 6: Mark

Staying in John Radcliffe hospital was the hardest night of my life. Jules had to go home, as no visitors were allowed overnight. She left with the family and I lay there just thinking, how, what, why? My head wouldn't switch off, but there was one thing that didn't change in my mind: I'm not having that operation. I will be fine. If I don't have it, the swelling could increase and I could have a seizure, fit or even die. If I have it, I could have a seizure, fit, contract MRSA during my 3 - 6 months in hospital plus be permanently disabled, lose my speech, memory and still die. The latter posed too many more risks.

Jules arrived there in the early hours of the morning and somehow sneaked passed security and crept into my room. I was so happy to see her! She laid next to me on the small hospital bed and we chatted quietly. I was still 100% confident that the operation wasn't necessary, and I would be fine. She agreed and totally trusted my instincts.

A few more blood pressure checks and other tests were done before the doc arrived. He was in a positive and happy mood as we walked into his office and I told him my decision. After a bit of interrogation, he agreed to let me go home under the condition that I did absolutely nothing for two weeks and returned for another scan.

It was such a relief to get home and sit in the garden for a while. My mum rushed straight down the road to see me and sat holding my hand so tightly that the pain in my head began to subside for a moment and I had to tell her to let go! More visitors arrived: my mum-in-law, sister-in-law and niece and nephew. It was lovely to see them and they all just hugged me. It's times like these that make you realise just how important family is.

Although it was a relief to be home, I still felt scared, in pain and unsure of what would happen next. Will I have a seizure? How soon can I get back to running and playing football? What if I never recover from this? Can I do my summer-school session in a few weeks? So many questions and no answers; there was only one thing for it. Sleep! I did what I was told (yes, really!) and took it easy.

You may think that this sounds crazy but after only eight weeks (and two CT scans) after my freak accident, I was totally discharged from John Radcliffe Hospital and told, live your life as normal! No need for any further treatment or life-threatening operations. I was told if my head hurts to take some painkillers or go to the GP. Wow, what a recovery, I thought. The only things I couldn't do were any contact sport and anything involving the risk of head injury (of course). Reluctantly I gave up playing football (which I wasn't great at but loved) however I was cleared to go running again (although the half marathon, called the Beast, I'd entered was quashed).

So, there you have it! That's the story! I'd survived against all odds and it was back to life as it was. Surely this should be the end of the book because you've read my fascinating story. Or is it just the beginning?

Do you know one of those blokes who won't go to the doctors when they're poorly or won't stop when they're tired because they're too manly or strong to admit defeat? Well I was one of those guys in a way.

I went home from John Radcliffe after the overnight stay and rested for a week. I felt rough, tired and weak but it gave me time to contemplate my options. I had some summer-school sessions booked in at a local school and then the new academic year started. September was a busy month with loads of bookings from the company I was freelancing with; I could do it! The survival adrenaline kicked in and I knew it would be a good earner. What's more, the best way to recover is to get on with it, so against all advice from my family and loved ones, I did just that and found myself travelling from Lincolnshire to Staffordshire to Liverpool in a week. I felt weak and emotional but the buzz of surviving and being alive took over.

Just before my third appointment at the hospital, I was starting to feel a bit vulnerable. The push of too much, too soon was starting to take its toll and I was panicking that at any moment I could have a seizure. Jules knew I was scared but also supported my every decision to recover without medical intervention. There were plenty of pleas for me to slow down but in my mind, I knew I needed to keep going, life went on.

At the end of September, we arranged a family get-together at our house and had a lovely Sunday dinner. It was really relaxed and everyone just enjoyed the time together. At the end of the evening my mum and nan left leaving just Jules, me and my mother-in-law Barbara (or Nanny to everyone). Jules left the room and Barbara came over to me, put her hand on mine and begged me to slow down. She also made me promise her that I'd send her a little message every day to tell her that I wasn't pushing myself. As she left to go home, she hugged Jules and turned and hugged me, giving me the, '*you'd better do as I say or you're in trouble*' look. I smiled a huge smile, Barbara was the one of the loveliest and most caring people in my life and once I'd made her a promise, I knew I couldn't break it. She hugged us both again, gave us her sweet smile and left for home.

Chapter 7: Jules

We tried our best to carry on as '*normal*', but we were so very mindful of everything Mark did and made sure he got plenty of rest when needed. I did worry that he was spending too much time on the laptop or mobile and was starting to push himself when he should be resting. I noticed the cracks were beginning to show in his personality.

The last Sunday of September was such a lovely day, it had been Mark's mum's birthday, so we had all of the family round for the day including my wonderful mum. I've always been close to my mum and often described her as the closest thing to an angel on this earth. She was sweet, caring, loving, selfless, quiet but one of the strongest ladies I know. I say lady, as she was truly a lady, I think I only ever heard her swear three times my whole life! We ate, we drank (tea!), we talked and, god, we could all talk and then early into the evening my mum hugged us all, said her goodbyes and left to go and watch the golf Ryder Cup. I phoned her the following morning and laughed that we had somehow managed to pull it out of the bag and beat the Americans; she was so happy about that! We chatted some more, I said goodbye and that I'd give her a call the next day as usual.

The next day I called as promised but didn't get any answer, so I just thought she must be out and I'd call again later. It was teatime and I was still at work, on the phone, when I noticed a call from my sister come up on my mobile. I finished my call and was about to ring her back when my son Daniel called.

"Have you spoken to Aunty Woo?" (his name for my sister, Lou) he asked.

"No, I was just going to call her back. What's up?"

'Nanny's dead mum! Woo went around to see if she was alright and found her."

WTF! All I remember him saying was that he was on his way to my office and then hung up. There was this almighty screaming noise and banging on the desk. It took me a little while to realise that it was me screaming and banging my fists on my desk,

"NOT MY MUM, dear god no not my mum!!!"

We all made a hasty trip to meet Lou who was still at Mum's house. I was calling my brother, Russell, my sister; I even asked her if she was sure Mum's dead.

She yelled back "For god's sake, yes she's fucking cold and stiff."

I hung up and carried on crying, debating with myself whether this was actually happening. Poor Mark was driving and trying to hold everything together and concentrate on getting us there. I'd phoned him on my way home from work to make sure he was there and said I was on my way. He knew something serious was up and when I got in and told him, he was as stunned as we were.

I went upstairs to where my mum lay. The ambulance staff had picked her up off the floor of her bedroom and put her on the bed covered with a sheet. I pulled it back and couldn't understand, couldn't take it in. There she was, dead, my sweet, sweet, caring, loving, angelic mum, dead. My mum, who was always there for me, who I rang every day, who I went to see, who met me at lunchtimes from work. No goodbyes, no final hugs, no nothing, just dead.

A numbness came over me as I tried to process this, the police came and took a statement from Lou and then they came to take her body. The pain that was now running through my every vein was so intense and my stomach felt like it was tied in a million billion knots and I couldn't breathe. There she was being carried out of her home in a black bag, the police went, and we're left in an empty house where our mum had taken her final breath, all alone. I was beyond grief; I was in shock, devastated beyond belief, what the hell just happened?

I've no idea how we all got through the next few weeks. I was allowed three weeks off work. I stayed with my sister intermittently, she'd found my mum, how was she ever going to get over that? The funeral came and went, everything was just a haze of immense sadness and loss, the grief was all-consuming. We'd lost our dad some 11 years earlier rather quickly but bless her, my mum's departure gazumped him; I'm sure that made her smile. I felt for the first time completely alone. Yes, I had Mark and our wonderful family, but no parents. It really was the emptiest place I think I've ever been in and no way of changing it.

I sat outside in our garden drinking tea on a cold bright early October morning considering all that had just happened in the past two months; how my life had changed drastically and what was really important now. I'd nearly lost my husband and lost my mum in such a short space of time. It made me re-evaluate everything. I ran inside to Mark and said, 'That's it, I'm leaving my job, I don't want to go back to all that stress and very long hours.' He hugged me and said 'Thank fuck for that.' He'd seen the toll it was taking on me. My plan was to join Mark in our businesses so we could spend more time together; that and the fact I could keep an eye on him too and help in his recovery.

We'd had another appointment at John Radcliffe and a further scan that showed the bleeds on both sides of the brain were going down. Great news! They signed him off as fit and well to get on with life. We're so grateful at this point that Mark is still alive, still able to fully function. There were still some side effects, like getting tired really easy, lack of concentration, memory loss, but we were confident that with his recovery so far, everything would be back to '*normal*' very soon.

I handed in my notice on the day I returned to work and felt a sense of relief and knew I'd made the right decision. I loved my job and the people I worked with, they were a fantastic team I'd put together, but the long hours and stress were things I'd come to realise over the last two months I no longer needed in my life. My directors and staff were shocked to begin with but understood how painful and difficult the past months had been and that being at home working with Mark was the right step to take. I had to work three months' notice due to being senior management, but I got through it.

Christmas came and it was just sad and empty. It was a time of year we all usually looked forward to; getting together, eating, drinking, and generally having lots of fun and games. But this year was so very different, we were all dreading it knowing there was going to be an empty seat at the table, a very much missed person wasn't going to be with us. The whole family congregated at ours and held each other up, there was laughter but there were also many tears.

Chapter 8: Mark

Two days after hugging Barbara the most awful, devastating thing happened. That smile she gave me turned out to be the last time I would ever see my beautiful mother-in-law smile. What the hell just happened? Barbara went home absolutely fine and passed away suddenly the next night. Bang! Just like that. We were naturally devastated.

The next few weeks were an absolute blur as the family tried to come to terms with what had happened. Jules spent a few nights at her sister's, and I remember feeling totally helpless. My head was throbbing constantly, but this seemed totally insignificant now. Nothing made sense. A huge loss of a loved one never does. In fact, tears are rolling down my face just remembering this and I'm struggling to write much more about it because it's too painful, still now.

All I'll say is that Barbara was the most caring and lovable mother-in-law that I could've ever wished for. Every moment with her was a joy. In fact, she brought pleasure to everyone in our families. We'd enjoyed some beautiful times with her, like trips to Spain where she'd always get stopped at security in the airport and take the heaviest ever suitcase just for a week. We'd sit and help her with the Sunday crossword and we'd never cheat on the internet. She brought absolute joy to me as a son-in-law and I was heartbroken. If I was heartbroken, you can't imagine how this hit Jules, the lads, my brother and sis-in-law and nieces and nephews!

It was a blur and I can't remember the order of events around this time. We'd made the final trip to John Radcliffe eight weeks after my accident and was told to live my life as normal, but it wasn't that easy. Jules and I sat in a pub in Oxford and ordered the worst pub meal ever. The food was terrible, the service not much better and the feelings were mixed. I'd just been signed off from the hospital which meant I'd made the right decision not to have the operation, but the loss of Nanny Barbara just pushed aside any feelings to celebrate.

December passed in a daze. We pulled Christmas crackers as we ate our Christmas dinner. The family were together and staying strong. However, one very special person from our lives was missing on this festive day. It was hard not to shed tears as we all sat together over a bowl of Christmas pudding.

Jules and I put on brave faces and tried to pick up life where we'd left it some four months earlier. I was nervous in busy environments and my head still felt sore. The emotion of losing a loved one would just hit me, but I couldn't cry when I wanted to. Jules had quit her full-time job as a training manager, much to my delight. We'd learned the lesson that we needed to remove some unnecessary stress from life and start living on our terms. We didn't want a boss saying you must do this and do that or someone dictating what we should or shouldn't do. So, Jules worked her final week of the three-month notice period after Christmas and came to join me in our businesses.

As well as the training business, I'd also joined a network marketing company. The plan was for me to continue travelling to schools and running the sessions. Jules would look after the network marketing Discount Club side of our business where we help people save money. We also had a nutrition business sandwiched somewhere in between. I was doing my best to convince her that all these ventures would somehow work and we would be buzzing and loving life again soon. To be honest I think I was trying to convince myself too.

Now I have to say that Jules is an extremely strong person and she held absolutely everything together amazingly. She's always been the glue in the family and when crisis hits, she is wonderful at calming situations down and dealing with things logically. We worked together on my recovery and Jules kept me in line, making sure I didn't do anything stupid (and most of the time I listened) and encouraged me in everything I did. As the months passed, I felt stronger and stronger, but I didn't want to admit that something still wasn't quite right.

Chapter 9: Jules

I left my job in February 2013. It snowed heavily on my last day and we'd planned a big celebration but the weather scuppered that. It was just as well. I was still an emotional wreck, feeling ok one minute then feeling like I'd been hit by a massive truck right in my gut, the next.

It was agreed with my family for me to take charge of sorting out Mum's estate as I now had more spare time and I set about doing that. It wasn't easy! I had to see solicitors, go to court, fill in copious numbers of forms, set up a bank account, speak to her bank and so much other stuff, then eventually arrange for the house to be sold along with sorting through all her belongings.

This all took time as you can imagine and Mark, god love him, was trying his hardest to carry on as if he hadn't had the accident. He was going up and down the country delivering motivational workshops in school to teenagers but was starting to find it tougher to concentrate for long periods. I also began to notice changes in his personality. He was becoming snappier and sharper with me, which wasn't like the old Mark at all. He'd shout me down if I tried to suggest something or maybe even if I just asked him what he was doing. More often than not he wouldn't wait until I'd even finished the sentence and he would bite my head off.

He would be working on his laptop and would suddenly explode with temper and annoyance that it hadn't gone as he'd wanted. He also started to do what I can only describe as fixate on things, and you couldn't change his way of thinking. It was like it was stuck in his mind and that was it.

This wasn't like Mark. Anyone who knew him would say he was the most laidback, horizontal, chilled out person they'd ever met. Nothing ever fazed him, he really did just love enjoying life and was always great fun to be around.

The changes were gradual and definite, but I was wrapped up in my grief and sorting out Mum's estate, so maybe I had missed some signs. We both decided that a break away would do us the world of good. There had been so much pressure on us both that it was no wonder the stress had taken its toll. We booked a trip to Thailand for June and began counting down the days until we'd be relaxing on the beautiful beaches with not a care in the world. That was how our life had always been: carefree. I missed that. We both had some concerns about how Mark would be on the 12-hour flight but thankfully he *'flew'* through it.

We just loved Thailand; we'd booked a package tour that started in Bangkok which was amazing, and we stumbled across a place called Nana and had a crazy night. There were bars, clubs, strip joints, lady boys, everything you could imagine. We were sitting at one of the bars chatting, laughing, kissing and the chap who was singing dedicated a song to the newlyweds, meaning us! We laughed and told him we'd been married almost nine years; I think he was a little shocked as to how close we are.

We went on to a place called Krabi and although the weather wasn't great for a few days, we managed to go and visit some amazing islands.

We then moved onto Phuket and stayed in the most wonderful little area right at the very bottom. The hotel was very colloquial and beautiful; it was so very peaceful and relaxing. We found a place called Russell's Sunset Bar! It was Mark's birthday while we there and we went on a tour to James Bond Island, which was fitting as Mark's a huge fan. That evening we went to Russell's bar; lo and behold, it was the owner, Russell's, birthday too! Needless to say, the evening was fantastic. We'd made friends with some other couples who were staying in the same hotel as ours who also frequented the bar. We all ended up at one of Russell's millionaire friend's mansion up in the hills playing silly games in his pool. It really was such a lot of fun and what a birthday treat for Mark, one he'll never forget! We got back to the hotel for breakfast and crashed out in bed for a few hours! We made a commitment that day to go back there for

Christmas. The couples we'd befriended already had their tickets and hotels booked so that was it, we'd join them for Christmas at Russell's.

It felt so good to have the chilled and carefree Mark back, but once we arrived back home, the difference in his personality all came flooding back. There seemed to be a little darkness creeping in around Mark. He had a reluctance to be with other people and certainly not near crowds. We'd already started to change our social habits and tried to go to places where there wasn't too much loud noise or big crowds. He seemed to be shrinking and becoming scared of trivial things.

I suggested we go back to see his neurologist, which we did in the September, where we discussed what was happening and how concerned I was about the changes in him. The neurologist, a nice guy, listened and told us it can take at least three years for things to settle after such a traumatic head injury and that what we were experiencing was normal. He even wrote in his letter to our GP that these symptoms should disappear in time. So off we went again, thinking ok, everything's going to be great.

But it wasn't, Mark wasn't coping. I didn't really know what was wrong. He was struggling to maintain a full day, he was tired, irritable, forgetful, snappy and he wasn't Mark anymore. It was hard to try and talk to him, but when I did, he was in denial and I just felt frustrated. I wanted to help, what I thought was helping, but it didn't make any difference. We'd been invited to a few great social events, like a fancy-dress bus day in London, but we had to turn it down even after I'd bought my costume (I was kinda looking forward to that).

He was pushing himself with work and travelling the country, then doing his running. I could see the effect this was having on him. No matter how many times I tried to talk and get him to see what was happening he wouldn't listen. At the very least he'd mumble something along of the lines of '*Oh, ok I'll try and get some rest*' or '*I'll try and eat more often*'.

He'd entered the Northampton Half Marathon, which was in the September, something he was really looking forward to. Running was a big passion of his and he felt it was a release for him and his changes. I didn't completely agree, as I could see how he was constantly pushing himself and felt like maybe he should moderate this for the time being. I often noticed after he'd been for a longish run that he looked different. His left eye always looked very large and glazed over and he would struggle to focus properly for a day or so after too. He always said '*nothing's wrong*' or '*I feel fine*'.

The race didn't go as planned, in fact it was probably one of the worst ones he's ever had. He'd had to stop, he'd felt ill, had no energy and thought he was going to pass out. He came home completely deflated and just collapsed asleep in the conservatory. I remember thinking, shit if this is now affecting his running then things must be really bad, but what am I going to do? We'd just seen the specialist and he told us everything was normal and this would pass in time. So I guess we just clung to this and hoped everything would just get better.

Another Christmas came and as I mentioned earlier, we went back to Thailand. Mark always seemed to be relaxed there, more than anywhere to be honest, and I hoped this break would do him good. Work was really beginning to take its toll on him and the company he was freelancing with had also noticed changes in him and his lack of energy in his delivery of the workshops. They had a few discussions with Mark and we tried to iron out the problems. Travelling by train was a good option to lessen the level of concentration required from driving. I really hoped this would solve some of the issues.

The beginning of 2014 was pretty busy; Mark had quite a lot of school work and as all of Mum's estate had been wound up, I'd begun to join him on some of the trips. This was mostly to help out with the driving, as this was causing a huge issue with his concentration and tiredness. He was beginning to look a bit thinner and seem to have a worriedness (if there is such a word!) about him that was never there before. He wouldn't tell me much about how he was feeling other than '*yeah I'm ok*'. It was still a problem to broach any subject of his well-being or mental state. He wouldn't accept anything was happening, wouldn't accept any advice or would agree half the time just to shut me up! I was beginning to get a little frustrated, as I wanted to help him and understand how he was feeling. I remember we were driving somewhere, and I was trying to explain how low I felt at that point. I was struggling to come to terms with working from home and spending lots of time on my own, something I'm not accustomed to. His reaction was just to bite my head off me and tell me what I was doing wrong or what I should've been doing and just to get on with it. There was little understanding or compassion from him. I was trying to hold back the tears whilst driving and feeling even lower than before. Where had my loving and understanding husband gone? I missed him. In fact, I missed us.

Chapter 10: Mark

It was a beautiful sunny evening when The Nutty Boys arrived in town. Yes, the amazing band Madness were playing at The County Ground in Northampton. This was such an exciting day; not only did we have tickets for the gig, but it was also the date of the first ever Northampton Half Marathon. Being a Northampton boy and proud of my roots, this was an ideal day for me, and I'd been beside myself with excitement for weeks. Now I know that running a half marathon isn't everyone's idea of fun, but it was certainly a rush for me. Jules was buzzing too, as we were meeting some friends in the afternoon and making a whole day of it.

"Go on Mark! Looking good mate! Wow there he is!" came the cheers from the crowd.

The race was wonderful. For a moment I felt free. Running through town past all those places I know from my childhood, seeing all the familiar faces cheering on the route. This was like running heaven to me.

But then, what the hell just happened? I woke up laying on the sofa in the conservatory and Jules was in the kitchen. She was a little annoyed at me and I was trying to work out why. I'd woken in a daze and tried to remember everything before I'd lain down.

At mile ten of the half marathon I'd gotten to the top of a hill and threw up. My legs were like jelly and I couldn't understand why. My arms were shaking as I began to walk again before slowly breaking into a light jog and picking up my pace.

"You ok mate?" came a concerned voice from a fellow runner. I carried on and tried to shrug it off. A mile later I was sitting on a grass verge with my head in my hands and shaking uncontrollably. I couldn't work out what was wrong, this was my hometown half marathon and I'd prepared properly beforehand. Not being defeatist, I got up and started to run again but every time I got into my stride, my legs just went to jelly. Declining lifts from concerned passers-by, I chose to walk to the end of the race in the beautiful Delapre Park. For the first time in my life I understood what a panic attack was.

Sitting underneath a tree looking across at my running club buddies smiling, I just wanted to cry. It didn't make sense, here was a high energy day but I felt so low. So alone. Why? I'm doing something I love, there are some good friends about and I'm in my hometown which I love.

I snuck off without anyone noticing and walked home. Feeling absolutely dejected, I told Jules that I'd felt sick and went to lie on the sofa.

Now, my wife knows me well enough to know that I hadn't just been sick, so she left me to sleep it off. When I woke, I could tell Jules was upset. We were supposed to meet friends an hour ago and we had to miss them. That was it, time for a pity party. The day felt ruined, the run was something special to me and the night was our night. The tickets to the gig were on the side in the kitchen, so I tried to get Jules to feel sorry for me, but she doesn't do pathetic.

I had been pushing myself too much again, trying to cram too much in and most importantly, ignoring everyone's advice to slow down. I went upstairs to get changed out of the running kit I was still wearing and sat on the edge of the bed. Suddenly I cast my mind back to that very last moment that Barbara, our Nanny, gave me that loving plea to slow down. I wanted to cry but nothing came out. Throwing my running shirt on the floor, it suddenly happened again. My arms shook, my legs went to jelly, and my head spun. My breathing felt as if it was stopping and my heart raced. Panic attack number two! The anxiety hit the roof! I was scared, angry, upset and just needed something or someone to stop this. I needed sympathy, pity... anything. My world felt terrible, I'd ruined a great day and I'd let everyone down.

What could've been minutes or even hours later, I woke up lying on the bed. I looked down and I was still in my running shorts.

The world seemed a bit calmer, so I got ready to go and watch Madness. Jules was downstairs and I could see she was upset. I picked up the tickets and suggested that we go, convincing her I was fine. Inside I was hurting, and we hugged for a moment. I tried to apologise and made some kind of excuse in an attempt to hide the panic attacks and feeling of anxiety. I thought, "I'm fine, honestly, I am... I'm strong and I'll recover from this one-off blip."

We went to Madness and watched from the back of the arena. It was a brilliant gig, but I was gutted that we'd missed out on all the fun with our friends. The guilt was somewhere deep as I tried to pretend that everything was fine and nothing had happened but inside, I knew something was wrong.

A couple of weeks before the Madness weekend, I'd been to an appointment with a neurologist consultant at Northampton General Hospital. After visiting my GP, he'd referred me for a scan to check the state of my brain and to see if the blood clot (subdural haematoma) had dispersed fully.

As I stared around the walls of the waiting area in the old hospital building, Jules and I sat in anticipation. There was a feeling inside that I should've made a full recovery by now and life should be back to where it was a year ago. Do you sometimes feel that you put a timescale on things and expect that overnight, a magic switch will flick into action? Well that was me. I'd been given recovery timescales of a loose six months and double that time had now passed.

I felt I was back into the swing of things. I was busy, delivering workshops in schools around the country and driving here, there and everywhere. I'd also run the Paris Marathon and passed my advanced driving assessment. We'd also visited Thailand which was my first trip on a plane since the accident and Russell had gotten married to Roxanne. It was great to be travelling again. Paris we did by Eurostar so there was no flying involved but Thailand was a 12-hour flight and I was a little apprehensive at first. My main worry was, would the air-pressure on the plane be too much? It was fine and the whole trip was an incredible relief. In fact, it was what we both needed.

However, there were a few concerns. Jules wasn't missing working full time but was struggling to adapt to not having a routine. After sorting out her mum's estate and helping Russ and Roxanne plan their wedding, she was sort of stuck in the background of our business.

I did my best to be my usual positive, laid-back self and live life at 100 mph. Truth be told, I began hiding a few things from Jules and myself. One day I made a trip from a school in Birmingham down to Devon. The school day finished at lunchtime and as I drove along the M5, I felt so tired that I pulled into a service station for a rest. After grabbing some food, I sat in the car, wound my seat back and closed my eyes. Waking up, I felt dazed and looked at the clock. Realising that I'd been in the services for nearly two hours, the parking time was almost up. Starting the engine, it was time to get back on the road and push on, otherwise it would be a crazy parking fine. Less than 20 miles later was the next services, so I pulled in there and slept for another 90 minutes.

Arriving at a lovely hotel in Honiton, I called Jules and told her what a great day I'd had at the school. We chatted for a while on the phone and then she told me to go and get food. Instead of heading downstairs to the dining room, I slept for another 45 minutes.

Back in the waiting area, we were called into the consultant's office and greeted by a friendly and calming welcome. He was really empathetic as he went through the results of the scan. The whole appointment was a bit of a blur, but I vividly remember him turning to Jules and saying, "You just want your husband back, don't you?"

I almost cried. Jules looked at me with deep love in her eyes, but I couldn't contemplate that I was a different person. A week later, a letter arrived with the following paragraph in it:

"He hasn't fully recovered. For most of the time he is now normal, but there are times when he's not quite right. He can be emotionally labile at times and may not be able to concentrate. His wife has been worried about him. He had a further head scan in June of this year and although it is reported to be showing a degree of right temporal lobe gliosis, it looks pretty normal to me."

The following line said that I'm living a pretty normal life as a motivational speaker, so I decided to carry on doing just that. This means it must be beatable and all the personal development and positivity in our lives means I didn't need to really worry about the rest of the letter.

The letter continued to say that it is still early days of recovery and things could continue to improve in a couple of years or so. There was a suggestion of a head injury clinic and visiting the charity Headway.

The final paragraph said, "Matters were looking good and there was a scar on my brain which could increase the risk of a fit, but it would probably never happen."

Being a glass-half-full type of guy, I focused on the positives; he used words like "optimistic" and "further recover" so surely time would be a healer. I decided not to follow up the referral to Headway and push on as before.

Reading the letter from the consultant, it seemed as if it would be a matter of time before a full and complete recovery would be achieved and there would be nothing to worry about. Broken bones mend and scars heal and so on.

More freelance work poured in and more journeys up and down the country. Plenty of sleeps in motorway service stations continued. March was always crazy around exam time and one week consisted of Corby on Monday and Dudley on Tuesday. After the school day finished in Dudley, I drove straight to Wales for a Swansea school on Wednesday and then it was on to Cardiff for Thursday.

That evening, I drove from Cardiff to Manchester for the final gig at a school in Sale. As soon as I got onto the M5, I rang Jules and we chatted on the phone until I pulled into the hotel car park in

Manchester. I was physically and mentally exhausted and the whole right side of my head ached as I slumped on the bed at around 9:00pm. I didn't like to stay away from home for one night so from Tuesday to Friday was too long and I knew something had to change.

The Sale school was quite a fun day; I learned that Cristiano Ronaldo had studied English there briefly when he signed for Manchester United.

Hopping in the car, it was time to dig in and battle the M6 to get home as soon as I could. Arriving home, I turned the key in the front door and felt relieved to be back. I heard Jules run into the hallway to greet me and we just hugged for ages before heading to the living room and slumping onto the sofa to catch up on the week's news.

I'd already decided by this point that something needed to change but what came next was not the change I had expected.

Chapter 11: Jules

Towards the end of March, Mark had work bookings all around the country, so we decided he would stay in hotels to ease the long days and I would get on with things at home. It meant being away from each other for a few nights, something neither of ever really liked doing but needs must and all that.

I laid in bed on one of the evenings when he was away, watching some crap on the TV and without realising, I was doing the womanly check-ups we're all told to do. Hang on a minute. What's that? I felt the colour drain from my face as I found what felt like a lump in my right breast, yep it was definitely a lump of some kind, shit! I decided to wait and see if was still there in morning; yep it was still there. Ok, let's see if it's still there tonight when I go to bed; yep it's still there, fuck.

Next morning, I phoned the doctor and went to see him. On examining me he said, "Yeah, there's definitely something there but it's not presenting itself sinisterly, however I do want you have a mammogram to be on the safe side." This was booked for about 10 days later.

Mark got back from his huge week of travels on the Friday night of that week totally exhausted and wiped out, so we just tried to relax. I kept thinking I need to tell him what's happening but I'm not quite sure how to start the conversation. Saturday evening came and we lay on the sofa and I just said, "I've got something to tell you."

"Ooh, is it exciting?" he replied.

"Erm, no."

He'd got a school booking on the day of the hospital scan but Daniel, our eldest son, was free and could come with me.

On the day of the mammogram, I was examined firstly by one of the head consultants who repeated that my *'lump'* felt and presented itself like a cyst and that she didn't think there was much to worry about, yippee!!! I texted this info to Mark so that he wasn't worrying and went off for the scan.

Once it was done, they straight away wanted to do an ultra-sound scan and I got ushered into another room. I could see the screen and watched as they performed it and I remember seeing what I thought was small dark mass. They then told me they needed to do a biopsy. Afterwards, they cleaned me up and I went back into the waiting room where Daniel was.

"All ok?", he asked. "You've been gone a while."

I told him what had just happened and then picked my phone up to find a few messages from Mark. Bugger, what am I going to tell him, I don't want him worrying. He's supposed to be motivating teenagers in a school and needs all his energy and concentration for that. I told him they're just being ultra-careful and taking some more tests and that I'm sure all will be fine.

I knew deep down it wasn't going to be fine, I had that awful gut feeling, but what could I say to him? Lying wasn't something I did but I just couldn't tell him the whole truth, not right now.

I was called through and taken to an office with three consultants and lots of screens in it. They showed me the results of my mammogram and the lump that I'd felt was there to be seen. They said they didn't think that it was anything too much to worry about, however underneath it was that horrid small black mass I'd seen earlier. This, they said, pointing to it, does concern us and looks particularly sinister. I now despise that word. I was given an appointment for three days later for the results of the biopsy and made my way back to the waiting room to see my beautiful son Daniel patiently waiting. My stomach was churning, my mind whirring, I felt so sick. I was sweating, shaking and scared, oh my god I was so fucking scared.

Those three days were particularly hard; the waiting always is. Sleeping was difficult and fitful for both of us. There wasn't anything we could do to hurry it up. I instinctively knew I was in trouble but we somehow managed to get each other through it.

There we were, sat in the Integrated Surgery department of the hospital, waiting to be called for the results. The place was full. Full of lots of women all looking as pale and petrified as me and, one by one, we got called through. Eventually after over two hours of waiting (yes, over two hours of torture for your mind to be thinking up all sorts of horrors) we got called through and saw the same consultant lady whom I'd met on the day of the scans.

We sat down and she confirmed that the original lump I'd found was indeed a cyst and nothing to worry about, but the little black mass was. They asked me what I thought it was. I replied, "It's cancer, isn't it?"

"Yes", she replied.

That's it, it's out in the open. I've said it, it's real, I have cancer. This shit is real.

My appointed nurse asked me, "Are you ok? You're not reacting how we'd expect you to right now."

I put my left arm and leg out to catch Mark as he's almost passing out and falling off his chair onto the floor, "I have to catch him first", was my reply to her.

This is his worst nightmare that one of us would get cancer or something similar and yes, here we are, it's happening, I have Grade 3 metastatic aggressive breast cancer.

My emotions kicked in, the tears were flowing and the questions started coming. Do I need chemo? Will I lose my hair? Will I need radiotherapy? Am I going to live? The answer was mostly yes apart from I didn't require radiotherapy. The dates were booked for my operations; first to have some lymph nodes removed to detect if the cancer was spreading; then for a full mastectomy and I was able to have reconstruction at the same time. I was thinking that this is good, only two operations to do it all, fewer things to go wrong. I wish!

On the way home I bought a big bottle of Jack Daniels; I needed something to try and calm me and the absolute terror that was running through me. We sat in the conservatory crying and hugging. How could this happen? Why me? Haven't we already got enough to deal with? Oh shit, how do I tell my kids, what do I say to them?

A huge sense of guilt swamped me, '*I'm sorry*' I kept saying. I felt like I'd let everyone down and ruined all our futures, but my wonderful, caring, beautiful hubby keeps hugging me and telling me to stop apologising. I plucked up the courage and phoned the boys and remember saying to Russell that I haven't even seen my grandkids yet!

He drove down from Darlington immediately and Mark picked up Daniel. Then we all hugged, cried and talked. As we went to bed, the boys did what they invariably do on occasions like this, they went out until the early hours and got horrendously drunk, love them!

The following days we had the ordeal of telling family. I wanted to keep this fairly low key and just get on with it and do what I had to do to rid myself of this awful disease. I wondered what I'd look like with no hair and then my awesome brother turned up. I looked at him and burst out laughing, he's naturally bald now and I just thought, '*Oh yeah, that's what I'm going to look like!*'

The operations went well and according to plan, my nodes were free of cancer, yay! I now had an implant where my booby used to be. After much soul-searching my intentions are to meet this challenge head on. I can't change where I am so to me this is the only option, I need to get better for everyone. I started reading up on the chemo and what to expect and it filled me full of dread. The meeting with the oncology team to discuss the treatments just made me come home and be sick. How was I going to cope and get through this?

A week after the op and being signed off ready to begin the treatment, I woke up to see my scar had a hole in it!! It had split open and I was in a sheer panic that it was going to tear. For the next couple of weeks, the hospital kept trying to repair this. They even tried re-stitching it but it wouldn't settle. Another op was booked and, whilst I was awake and under local anaesthetic, they cut the whole scar back open, took some skin off each side and re-stitched it in the hope it would now heal fully. It did to a degree but as it was getting close to the point where I could no longer delay the chemo, my first session was arranged.

Chemotherapy for breast cancer is nothing short of brutal. My PICC line (a thin, long catheter) was inserted into my arm weeks beforehand in preparation. It was the most surreal experience watching those three vials of chemo being pumped into my body; one of them was red which made my pee red too. Bless her, my sister sat with us and we just watched. We all felt sick knowing what was happening. I got all my anti-sickness drugs, my steroids, my mouth washes, my medicine to make me poo, my thermometer and went home in trepidation of what this was going to do to me. By 9pm-ish I started feeling a bit woozy and went to bed. I woke the next morning thinking '*Oh god, I'm gonna be sick*.' I quickly got up and took my pills. Shit, I felt bad, I couldn't focus and my brain was total mush. I felt like I'd drunk a whole bottle of Jack Daniels and then been put on a spin-cycle in the washing machine! I just laid on the sofa in the conservatory and let it all wash over me. Knowing I've got another two more of these doses then three of some other drug, followed by 12 months of Herceptin injections, filled me full of absolute horror.

Poor Mark, I know he felt awful not being able to help. I'm a stubborn bugger when I'm ill and I just want to get on with it. He just sits and watches and I love him even more for that. I think about how he is and how he's going to cope. He's already doing way too much and the effects are really beginning to show. His forgetfulness causes much frustration. I'm beginning to lose count of how many times I've said '*I told you that earlier, or yesterday.*' He says he can't remember. I don't mind if it's something little, but when it's something important I need him to know, it's frustrating. I can't help but think '*Well you can remember anything to do with football but nothing I seem to tell you!*'

Joking apart, it really is becoming a bit of an issue, and I see him getting annoyed that he doesn't recall some conversations even if I tell him when, where and what we were doing when we had them. I've even begun to start doubting myself as to whether we've had the discussion or not and there are times now where I'm thinking maybe he's using the memory loss as an excuse as to why he hasn't done something I've asked him to do, or pick something up I needed? This makes me feel really bad. In the whole time of being with Mark I've never had to question anything and to be having thoughts like this now really hurt me.

The first week after chemo wasn't pleasant to say the least. I just rested, drank loads of water, took my pills and washed my mouth out regularly to try and avoid too many ulcers. Slowly I began to feel a little better and my energy levels started to increase. I'd been told during the 14 days after each chemo I'd be very susceptible to infection or catching the simplest of colds. So I took great care not to be in crowds and avoided anyone with the slightest hint of anything wrong with them. Day 12 after the first session I awoke feeling unwell with a headache and shivers. Mark went across the road to do his usual parkrun and I took my temperature. It spiked at 39 degrees so I rang the emergency number I'd been given and was told to make my way immediately to A&E.

I fetched Mark and off we went to the hospital. They checked me, gave me antibiotics straight away and I was admitted to an isolation ward specifically for cancer patients. I had some kind of infection, but we couldn't find the source, so I stayed in overnight. By the next morning I had found the source, my whole boob reconstruction area was red and hot, there it is! I showed it to the doctors and they confirmed indeed it was infected, but hopefully the intravenous antibiotics should sort it out.

A hole began to appear again on my scar. The nurses tried everything to try and patch it up but over the next day it grew bigger and the pain was now incredibly unbearable. I was putting wads of tissues around it to soak up the oozing puss that was coming out. I felt so ill and could hardly move for the pain. It was at this point I was made aware that I was neutropenic which meant I had no immune system left to fight any infection. If the antibiotics don't work my body will completely shut down; not a good situation to be in. It also turned out my consultant was away on holiday that week, so nobody was taking any charge of me.

Four days later and I was still in isolation, still in immense pain and now very tearful. I lost my temper and demanded I was seen. The other breast cancer surgeon consultant at the hospital eventually came to see me and took one look at my reconstructed boob and said we have to take it out because it's not settling. No shit Sherlock! I think even I worked that out! I was quite gutted by this. I'd struggled for weeks and weeks to get it to heal and constantly taking trips to the hospital every other day to get it checked and now to no avail. I was angry with my own surgeon, but to be honest I was just plain pissed off with life. The pain wasn't getting any easier and to make matters worse my hair had started to fall out in small handfuls too. How much worse could this get? Mark and my boys spent as much time as they could with me, and I could see the worry on their faces. Once again, there wasn't anything they could do. They were great though, trying to cheer me up, but I'm normally the one who holds everything together in a crisis. The cracks were beginning to show, and I honestly didn't know how much more strength I had within me. Was I going to break under the pressure?

Chapter 12: Mark

I felt sick as Jules told me that she'd been to the doctors that week to check out a lump she'd found on her breast. The doctor had said it was probably only a cyst but referred her to the hospital for a check-up. It would probably be fine, but my already increasing anxiety went through the roof. Statistics say that over 90% of things we worry about never happen, but this was far too serious not to be concerned about.

Two weeks later, we sat in a room at Northampton General Hospital to be told the devastating news that the initial lump was a cyst but the lump behind it was grade 3 breast cancer! After waiting for hours in the waiting room for a really late appointment, what we'd suspected was confirmed, and we were devastated. The consultant held her hand out to comfort Jules, but I almost passed out.

The consultant was naturally lovely and just held Jules's hand for a moment and said, "Don't worry, you're going to be fine, trust me!" Something in her voice seemed real, it wasn't as if she was just saying this as a comforting line.

We then had to talk about lots of options surrounding operations, treatments and so on. Within moments of receiving life-changing news like this, it's incredibly hard to make those decisions.

We went home, cried and then cried some more. We called the boys and then cried again. What the hell just happened? Why? How? Jules is a healthy person who looks after herself. She's fit and active and doesn't feel ill. It didn't make sense at all.

I went to pick Daniel up and Russell jumped in his car and drove from Darlington to Northampton immediately. It could be compared to the worst nightmare you've ever experienced but it was all too real.

The following day I had a school booking in Wolverhampton.

We decided between us that I should go, and the lads would look after Jules for the day and be there for her. It was horrible! I stood in front of a group of teenagers delivering a session on fun revision techniques but nothing about me could think of anything fun. I just wanted to be at home with Jules. Why am I here? All I could think about was my lovely wife at home. As the students worked on an example, I popped out to the toilet and was physically sick. I looked for every excuse I could think of to quit the session and go home, but ended up seeing out my commitment. The session was a complete blur.

The next few weeks consisted of telling people the news, dealing with their shock and preparing ourselves for a long road ahead. Operations, treatments like chemotherapy, hair loss, sickness... all these things were topics of conversation. The age-old saying of, you wouldn't wish this on your worst enemy (not that I feel we have any of them) is all well and good, but how could this happen to my wife? She is the most caring and selfless person ever, who looked completely fit and healthy. She doesn't deserve to go through something as horrible as this.

Being our usual positive selves, we decided to face everything head on. There isn't much choice in these situations. Do you understand how a rollercoaster works? Of course you do! Well this is how our life became now. The cancer had been caught early enough to be removed – great news. You'll still need chemo and that'll make you sick and you'll lose your hair – terrible news. You're eligible for a drug called Herceptin and that'll help to prevent any stray cells from returning – great news. Of course, nothing is guaranteed though and by the way, your next major operation will be delayed - terrible news. Don't worry though, everything looks really positive and trust me, you'll be fine – great news. The final statement was repeated by the consultant and nurses over and over again. We could do nothing but trust their message.

Almost two months to the day after Jules told me about the lump, we sat in the hospital for some more test results. Jules had had two operations since. The first was to have some lymph glands removed to see if the cancer was contained, and it was. The second was a full mastectomy and breast reconstruction. A male consultant sat down next to Jules's breast care nurse, and said,

"Well I have some news for you, the operation was a success and the tumour has been removed. That means the cancer has been removed."

Now my concentration and ability of being able to process information on the spot has been seriously affected since my brain injury but I think I knew what this meant.

"Could you repeat that please?" I asked.

The consultant did and asked me if I understood. I just replied that I wanted to hear him say again that the cancer had been removed. This was the best piece of news we'd heard since the horrible diagnosis. We almost floated out of the hospital smiling at everyone who we passed. Tears ran down our face and we went straight into town and celebrated by getting drunk. What else could we do?

I'd love to tell you that that's the end of that matter, but it wasn't. We knew the treatment was still to come. This was a safety net to do everything possible to prevent any chance of cancer returning. On top of that, a mastectomy takes a long time to recover from too. At this point though, that was in the future and this was the moment, it was time to enjoy the news and be positive. One day at a time, one step at a time, we would get through this.

Chapter 13: Jules

After days in isolation, crying with pain, the operation to remove my reconstruction went ahead. On waking in the recovery room, I felt absolutely amazing and even got told by one of the nurses, '*well you're far more alert than you should be!*' Although I'd been opened up yet again and stitched up, I felt a huge weight had been lifted and honestly the pain had subsided so much. Once I was back on the isolation ward, we even discussed me going home as I was so much better. However, as I had another drain in, it was decided that it was best to stay another night.

Once I eventually got home, I needed a shower and to sort my hair out. It was really long and I'd had it in a bun the whole time I was in hospital. I just wanted to wash it, feel clean and relax. I took the hair bobble out and went to brush it and the whole lot just fell onto the floor in one big lump! Boom, there goes my hair, I'm bald! I carried it downstairs to show Mark and we just stared at it for a while. We hugged each other and accepted it for what it was; another step on the long road to recovery. It felt very strange having no hair, but thankfully it actually quite suited me. There was something almost liberating about it, especially as it was summer.

It took another 10 days to get my immune system back up to re-start my chemo. I managed to get through the next two rounds although with another short stint in the isolation ward. Apparently, there was still some infection left which flared up due to the chemo, but with a load of antibiotics, I was home after a couple of days. Lou came to visit me in hospital with her children, Molly and Noah. My wonderful niece had brought me a lovely thick pair of socks to wear. Little did she know that I'd been so cold throughout the previous night that they were a godsend, what a legend she is!

Mark continued to keep our school business going, travelling up and down the country. I could see it was taking its further tolls on him. He looked tired but kept saying that he felt fine. I'd decided that, come what may, I'd make sure that everything is done so all he has to concentrate on is getting to the schools, delivering the workshops and getting home. I somehow managed all the housework, shopping, gardening and cooking etc. Cooking was hard, the chemo made my mouth extremely sore and everything I cooked just tasted like sour milk. Half the time when I came to eat, I just couldn't. The smell and taste made me feel sick. However, at least it was something less for Mark to think about. I even managed to get out for walks most days and had a few gym sessions too!

By now I had no hair anywhere on my body, even none up my nose which caused it to run all the time. No eyelashes made my eyes weep and the constant wiping with a tissue only made them sore. My lovely sis bought me some silk handkerchiefs to ease the soreness, how thoughtful! I really didn't like the way I looked, my face had a redness and bloating from the chemo and I just looked plain ill. I'd given up mostly on wearing any form of wig; they just drove me mad and were so uncomfortable. As it got colder, I resorted to wearing woolly hats, much nicer!

Then came the last three rounds of chemo which was just one vial of a drug called 'T' for breast cancer. I'd read up all about it and was really dreading it. To start with I was ok and then the pain set in. It was immense and nothing like I'd experienced before. It was in my neck and I thought it was my glands and I just couldn't move; it was excruciating. I took pain killers every two hours and just lay lifeless on the sofa for two days. Mark was beside himself with what to do, but there wasn't anything he could, except just watch me. Finally, I decided I needed help and went to the hospital. The doctor began to examine me and I let out a huge scream when he touched my neck; it felt like he'd put a big knife through it. He told me it wasn't my glands, it was my neck muscles and it was just a side effect of the chemo. All I could do was go home and continue with the pain relief. How long is this going to continue? Eventually it subsided after a couple of days. My god we were both dreading the fact I needed two more sessions of this drug, I really didn't want it to happen again but thankfully my body coped better with it and I got through. I did however require a blood transfusion as my count was very low. This really picked me up.

I was due to start the next year of my treatment on a drug called Herceptin. My oncologist had wanted to begin this with my first 'T', but I put it off until the second one in case I had a reaction to it. Once I'd been given this injection, I had to sit in the hospital for six very long hours while they monitored me, but thankfully there was no reaction.

December the 1st and the last 'T' chemo was administered along with my second Herceptin and the PICC line removed. That was such a big step forward, it meant I could have a proper shower or bath without having to wear a big plastic sheath to cover my arm, amazing! I could wear any clothes I wanted without worrying about catching it. I felt so good!

Halfway through the course of Herceptin, I was in a lot of pain in my hands, elbows, knees and feet. I just put it down to arthritis which I'd had in my hands for quite some time beforehand. However, this was pretty bad and each morning on waking it was incredibly painful to get up and get going. I had to hold each of my arms, as letting them fall straight was excruciatingly painful. Eventually as I slowly managed to get my body moving, the pain would get easier to bear. Then one of the nurses that came to administer my next Herceptin injection asked if I had any joint pain.

"Oh my god yes!" was my reply.

It turned out this was indeed a side-effect of the drug and once the course was complete, it would subside. I was hugely delighted to hear that and yes, even though I still have bad pains in my hands, the rest has mostly gone, hallelujah!

There were many long days throughout the treatment where I wasn't able to function like I wanted to. I'd take myself out of Mark's way and just watch TV in the hope that the next day I'd feel better. We managed to have some nice days out when I was feeling good, like a beautiful day in Stratford for example. We wandered around, fed the ducks and looked in the shops. I took a lovely trip up to

Darlington for a few days to visit Russell and, oh, the fudge we bought at the York Christmas fair; it was scrummy!

Lou did the most incredible thing; she had a sponsored head shave to raise money for Breast Cancer Research. It was a lovely evening made even more so as our cousin, Claire, was over visiting from New Zealand where she'd emigrated many years before. Lou raised just over £1,000 that night and made me be the first to start the shave off. It was so brave of her and I was so immensely proud.

Throughout this awful six months, Daniel, Russell, Lou and my brother, Warwick, were just amazing. They would call me every day and visit regularly. I know that without them I wouldn't have been as strong and both Mark and I are forever grateful to them for their support and love. Any time the pain or the enormity of the situation got me down, I'd tell myself over and over, this will pass. It had to, didn't it?

Chapter 14: Mark

I was lying in bed staring at the ceiling. Jules wasn't next to me; she was in hospital awaiting another operation the next day. I'd lost count of the number of operations now. She didn't deserve this. My lovely wife who is fit, active and healthy was now lying in a private room hooked up to a drip, feeling sick, in immense pain and her immune system had collapsed. A combination of chemo and a huge infection battered her body and caused it to fight to survive. After a few minor ops, the breast reconstruction didn't work, and a major operation was needed to remove it.

Deep down inside I knew everything was going to be ok, but it didn't stop the anxious wait and worry. I think fatigue finally overcame me and I woke the next morning.

The past few months I'd been on that crazy rollercoaster again. The consultant gave Jules a thumbs up to go away on holiday before her chemo started, so we booked a week in Menorca for my 40th birthday. The following day her reconstruction burst open and we had to cancel it. We did spend the weekend celebrating my birthday in London and packed in a few gigs seeing the Eagles, Iron Maiden, Metallica and Elton John (random combo there eh?).

Music is a real passion of ours, and this gave us a great escape from the stress and anxiety going on in the background. Earlier that year we went to see the Fratellis in Birmingham. It was a small venue with standing room only and we stood at the very back. Being part of the music crowd made me feel alive. I knew this was something that would bring me back to closer to my head-banging days before the day of banging my head.

Seeing the Eagles was a band that had been on my list since I was a kid. Mum had brought me up listening to them and the whole night filled me with so much emotion, as music can really touch your soul. Although I'm not sure how soul-touching Iron Maiden, Metallica and the other heavy rock bands are, we were buzzing and enjoyed every moment of this weekend called Sonisphere at Knebworth House.

It was back on the rollercoaster though. A low, followed by some highs and then a low again. Chemo and hair loss followed by sickness; it's horrible to see the person you love most in the world go through this.

Friday afternoon arrived and I got a call from the hospital to say Jules was in recovery and she'd be back on the ward. Dan, Russ, Roxanne and I arrived on the ward and Jules was a completely different person. She was sat up in bed and chattering like there was a year's worth of news to tell. The relief was immense as she was allowed home again and the intense pain had gone.

The chemo was horrible! The first three sessions were bad and the last three were worse than bad. Jules had another spell on the isolation ward at the hospital after developing another infection due to her low immune system. We counted down every treatment day in the chemo suite and moved forward step by step. Some days we'd do normal stuff and some days Jules would feel sick and rest. It was more than an emotional rollercoaster now, there was no way of describing it.

Every person I met asked, '*How's Jules?*' and then I'd have to relay the same story for the umpteenth time whilst on autopilot. Some friends we'd not seen for ages were there, doing everything they could to help and others didn't know how to cope and left us to it. It was bizarre. We didn't know how to cope at times, but others certainly didn't either, so they stayed away. One thing is for sure, Dan, Russ and Lou were there every step of the way. Jules is everything to them as she is to me, so we just wanted to do all we could.

Do you find that sometimes you have enough on your plate that you couldn't possibly have anything else? What happens next? Yep, something else gets thrown at you.

I was off to a school session just outside Warrington, while Jules went to hospital for another chemo session with Warwick, my brother-in-law. To ease the pressure of driving, I'd started to travel by train, which was making life a little easier.

The school session was a bit of a nightmare. It was very badly organised by the staff and the students were quite rude and disrespectful. This led to the day finishing a little earlier than expected which was a small result because it meant I'd get home earlier. I didn't like leaving Jules, especially while she was going through this awful treatment.

I stood on the platform planning my train connections. Warrington has two train stations: Warrington Central and Warrington Bank Quay, which are a mile apart. I had to make a short journey to Bank Quay, walk to Central and then travel home via Crewe. The train to Crewe departed Central about nine minutes after the first leg of the journey arrived. Now I always love a challenge so when the first train pulled into Bank Quay station, I stood by the exit door, backpack securely fastened and my hand hovering above the open button. The doors opened and I jumped off the train, dodged a couple of pedestrians and retraced my steps through the centre of Warrington back to the Central station. Sweating, I looked up at the clock on the platform and realised that I had two minutes until my Crewe train departed. I looked to my right and it was just pulling into the station. A few fellow passengers gave me a funny look as I punched the air in delight; I'd made it. Yep, those little victories in life!

When I got home, I went to check on Jules who'd only just gotten home from hospital. Before I could ask her how she was, she interrupted and told me to ring the doctor, now!

Only a week ago I'd had a horrendous pain in my right side and was struggling to breathe. The doctor referred me to the hospital for a walk-in x-ray, but I'd since felt fine. I knew it would be the results but, to my surprise, I was told to rush (carefully) to the hospital because I'd suffered a primary spontaneous pneumothorax. Ah ok, one of those... yep, I had no idea what this meant either.

Bless him, Warwick hopped straight back into the car and drove me to hospital. Thanks mate, great to see you and spend the whole day waiting in the hospital.

I soon learnt what a primary spontaneous pneumothorax is. Basically, my whole lung had collapsed on the right side and the nurse had to perform an aspiration. That involved sticking a very big needle in my chest and draining the air from between my chest wall and the lung itself. I'm shit scared of needles at the best of times so that wasn't pleasant.

The staff in A&E were fantastic and I had the biggest fitness ego boost I could ever receive. Firstly, I was told it's quite common in young, slim, fit and active men... ooh stop it! Next the nurse returned to the cubicle and asked if I was really 40 and not 25... thank you! Then I broke the news that not only had I run a 5K parkrun a couple of days earlier, I'd also run a mile in seven minutes between two train stations with a backpack on my back and a collapsed lung inside my body! Superman (or SuperMark) at your service!

After all the flattery and laughter, I was warned that this was actually quite serious and life-threatening if not treated. Oh c'mon, I don't need this in my life now, seriously! My wife's going through the worst possible treatment ever and I'm recovering from a brain injury. So, I decided, Jules was having enough of hospitals and I'd escaped one life threatening operation so this one simply had to be dealt with by healing itself. This time I'd listen to advice and follow the medics' guidance.

"Rest, don't run and if you need to get a train connection, next time use a taxi" was the last advice from the friendly nurse. "We'll see you in a week and will assess you then!"

Ok, so no running, no sprinting, no circuit training, no heavy lifting and very little walking was on order for the next week. I was scared of two things: the slim chance of being hospitalised for an operation and the absolute certainty of having another bloody great needle stuck in my chest in a week's time.

Thankfully after two more visits to Northampton General Hospital, my lung had repaired itself naturally and I was given the go-ahead to begin physical exercise again. What a relief! Talk about adding to the anxiety pot though. It was scary now having to wonder if my lung would collapse every time I either went for a run, did a gym session or picked up something heavy. The best way to deal with it was not to think about it too much so, as usual, I just decided to get on with life.

(N.B I did actually suffer another spontaneous pneumothorax about six months later and thankfully this repaired itself again).

"Everything will be fine now!" These are the words we kept hearing over and over again from everyone now Jules's chemo was finally complete. I was so relieved that we'd reached the end of that horrific treatment. Chemo destroys everything in your body physically and mentally and to see a loved one go through that is horrible. This is something that is supposed to make you better as well.

I was a little guilty too of thinking that everything would return to pre-diagnosis and we could get on with life again. Deep down I knew that it wouldn't be that easy, but I just wanted my confident, bubbly wife back now. The thing is, in a little over two years, I'd suffered a life-threatening brain injury and Jules was scarred from ten or so operations and being pumped full of different medications. Talk about in sickness and in health! We're a strong couple and we were doing our best, but had the damage from the stress already been done?

Chapter 15: Jules

Christmas 2015 and we all congregated at our house again with lots of talk of holidays and day trips for the New Year.

This was really hard for me. I was at my lowest point internally I've ever been in. I had no self-confidence; my hair was just starting to make a re-appearance, but it had left me feeling unsure of who I was anymore. I felt lost and I wasn't sure if I'd come back to the confident and carefree Jules I'd been before the cancer. I tried so hard to explain this to Mark, but I guess it's one of those things that unless you're there, you don't know what it's like or how it really feels.

Mark convinced me that a couple of weeks in Thailand was just what we needed. I wasn't so sure. I felt scared to be so far away from home and the hospital if I needed it. I didn't like people seeing me looking and feeling the way I did, and the thought of having to wear a bikini made me feel full of uncertainty. We went ahead and booked it. Although there were a few low times for me, like seeing lots of beautiful women with lovely boobs in bikinis, we were able to relax and enjoy our time away. I recall one day walking past a Thai massage parlour and hairdressers where a lady was calling out to any female passers-by if they wanted a haircut; she even asked me which we found funny, as there was nothing to cut! I recall the most amazing pancakes loaded with fresh coconut we had on pancake day and the silly sunglasses Mark had found discarded on the beach and wore for the whole holiday!

Mark enjoyed this short break and seemed to relax; we set some goals for the year including for him to complete 15 half marathons, crazy man!

As the worst of the chemo was over, I set about trying to get things back to normal. I did lots of networking for our home-based business and I joined the committee of a local British Legion and helped out with lots of fundraising for them. By now we were aware that we were going to be grandparents for the first time. Both our sons' partners were expecting with their due dates only four days apart! I know my boys do lots of things together, but this was something else. I was super excited!

As 2015 went on, Mark was generally very up and down. He was very stressed about lots of things, stuff that wouldn't have bothered him before. He was agitated about driving to the school bookings and spent a lot of time on the phone to the office that booked him. I was particularly worried about his obsession with this and asked him not to keep mentioning it to them as I felt they might stop using his services. We worked out ways of him going by train to the bookings or I would drive him. Those were always a bit difficult, as I had to find something to do whilst he was working. I did lots of shopping, walking and sometimes would find a leisure centre and go for a swim.

His love for life was definitely diminishing, and it was really hard to talk to about the differences in his character. He wouldn't accept that anything had changed and said that he was generally alright, but you could see that he wasn't really enjoying the school work as much as he used to. Before, he would come home full of energy and tell me all about his day, but now it would be about how it wasn't such a great session.

If I tried to talk to him about how he's now much more negative or stressed, he wouldn't let me finish my sentence. Half the time and would shout me down and say that I was wrong. He'd then go into a shell and be very quiet. He often complained of pain in his head where the fracture was and we tried to think that this was normal, but I could sense it was bothering him.

I could generally tell when things weren't good within him, as I could see it in his face. He would almost be a grey colour and his eyes would be kind of glazed over.

I remember one Saturday going to the gym; when I left, he was in good spirits and on my return, he was a completely different person. He was very quiet and withdrawn and it seemed like something was really bothering him. I asked him what was up, what had happened since I went out, but he couldn't answer me, he just mumbled that he was ok and off he went to the football. So, there I am again left wondering what the hell just happened.

Now that was something that used to confuse the hell out of me. We'd changed a few things that we'd normally do as he couldn't cope being in crowds or around loud noise, but he still managed to go the football with large crowds and noise. How could he cope with that? We'd turned down many invites from people because he didn't want to be in large groups or noisy surroundings; this just is not making sense at all. In June that year we went to Berlin for his birthday and to see AC/DC, huge crowds and of course very loud!

He kept training and running to complete his half marathon challenges and again I wondered how he was dealing with that. He would quite often be very tired afterwards and a big bone of contention was that he wasn't eating properly either and began to look thin. I know when doing lots of running and training, naturally you will lose weight, but he was skipping meals, particularly when he was in a school. I tried many times to get him to look at his eating and maybe change to eating smaller meals but more often. I could try and manage this while I was with him but even then, he wouldn't always eat everything given to him. Family and friends began to comment on how tired and drawn he looked and asking us if everything was ok.

He'd noticed that his freelance school bookings were becoming fewer than he'd previously been given which caused him huge angst. I would come in and he would invariably be on the phone to the office trying to figure it out. This left him quite unsure of himself and knocked his confidence even further. He didn't however talk that much about it to me, he would go back into his shell.

The end of October saw the birth of our darling granddaughter, Thea, and the beginning of November our wonderful grandson, Isaac. I was thrilled to bits! Mark was delighted too but having never had any babies of his own (his choice) he was a little nervous around them to begin with which is natural. They absolutely adore him now though!

I'd managed to talk Mark into going back to see his neurologist at the hospital in November, but again, as Mark was to all intents and purposes '*fully functioning*' there didn't seem much they could do. We were told once more that it can take years for everything to settle down and the consultant recommended he visit a local organisation called Headway for support and wanted to prescribe Mark anti-depressants. Well we both were adamant at the time he wasn't depressed! Yes, he was having some very dark days but was still managing to keep our school business going, along with our second part-time one helping people to save and make money (along with me of course!).

Not only that, we'd been on holiday to Thailand, we'd been to Corfu for a week with his dad, step-mum Katy and their son Ethan, and then to Berlin, Ischia & Sorrento and Lanzarote was coming up in December. Surely you can't be depressed if you can manage all this and the running. That's not depression, we said.

Lanzarote was another great holiday and Mark completed his final half-marathon! This seemed to be the best tonic for us both, being away. He lost a lot of his tension and was more open to talking. It was one of the first holidays where we spent hours just lazing by the pool while Mark researched the after-effects of brain injuries on the internet. We were still trying to come to terms with what had happened and how it had changed him as a person. It really began to throw some light onto what was happening and why it was happening. I could see that it was helping Mark get to grips with the enormity of the injuries he sustained, how he managed to survive but most importantly, right at that moment, what the future could be looking like for us. We began to understand a little bit more about why he suffered from memory problems, tiredness, mood changes, fatigue, the inability to concentrate or focus, the dislike of being in large or noisy crowds or even any form of background noise. We felt like we were finally beginning to make some progress in terms of how we can manage these situations in the future.

We also talked at length about the school work and how this was having an impact on it. He wasn't enjoying it as much as he used to. The company, who sent us the bookings, were beginning to notice the changes in him and his style of presenting their sessions. They'd called him to discuss a couple of issues, but Mark was struggling to come to terms with the negative feedback and how he could overcome it.

We came home feeling charged up and positive about the future, however under no illusion that it was still going to have its challenges. Mark wanted to strive to be more upbeat, not let things get to him as much and take the rest when needed.

2015 had been a strange year in that there were so many highs and so many lows. Life has a funny way of challenging you at times and my goodness, we'd been put to the test. Was it too much to ask to have a little less stress and a little more normality?

Chapter 16: Mark

My idea to get Jules's confidence back was to try and do everything at 100 mph. After a lovely Christmas Day with all the family and seeing in the New Year with Russ and Roxanne in Darlington; it was time to get on with our 2015 goals. Being in the business of personal development, we don't really do those sort of New Year's resolutions that nobody sticks to, we make proper goals.

Time to live life to the max! Let's get back to travelling, going to see bands and socialising. I set myself a goal to run 15 half marathons that year (15 in 2015).We booked another trip to Thailand plus tickets for AC/DC. The plans were exciting but, whilst I was starting to feel better in myself, Jules was struggling to go out in public. Her hair began to grow back, but her immune system was still weak.

We went to Thailand in February and it was a huge deal for Jules to pop a bikini on and sit on the beach while wearing a bandana. She'd always be beautiful to me, no matter what, but I understood how this dramatic change had knocked her self-esteem. She was also still on a year's worth of Herceptin treatment which involved an injection every three weeks. Yep, I decided not to watch that process. Although nowhere near as bad as chemo, this treatment still weakens the body and causes pain as a side effect. Not that we knew that at the time.

As the year went by, Jules got stronger both physically and mentally. It was mind-blowing and emotional to see her recover so well and so quickly, but I knew her confidence was still quite low. I'd had no further lung problems and was running well in my half marathon quest, recording three personal bests that year. On the family front, Dan and Russ both became parents. Their children, Thea and Isaac, were born within weeks of each other. It brought us great joy becoming Nanny and Pappa but, despite my elation, I still couldn't shake this relentless tired feeling.

I'd made the decision to continue doing as much of my travel to schools by train, meaning I could switch off on journeys. It was a little better, but something still didn't feel right. Family and friends kept commenting that I wasn't quite the same. It didn't make sense though. I was still running both of our businesses with Jules, I felt fitter than ever before, but I was struggling to focus. People commented that I was losing weight. How? I was eating. People commented that I was quiet. Why? Life was good. Jules had told me she felt frustrated at times because I didn't listen to what she was saying. We'd have conversations about something, important or trivial and I'd have little recollection of the facts.

To be honest, I didn't realise how different things were. Aside from the ongoing tiredness and dull pain in my head, I thought I could keep shrugging things off. Three years had now passed since my accident and I continued to look forward in life. Some of these things that people were describing about me didn't sound like me, so I dismissed most of them. I felt like I'd come such a long way. Maybe I did need some extra help but, I'll be honest, I found it hard to ask for it.

Do you ever get that moment when you think it's time to swallow your pride and listen to your wife (or partner/mum/dad/family – depending on your circumstances)? Well after about the third or fourth suggestion, I booked an appointment with my doctor. He referred me to the neurologist, who referred me to Headway (a charity that works to improve life after brain injury). He also suggested I went back to the GP for anti-depressants. I was discharged again but told that I'd be welcome back should the need arise.

I spoke to Jules after my appointment and told her ok, I'll go to Headway but I'm not taking anti-depressants. Lots of friends have tried them with adverse effects. I'm not depressed, and I don't need them. Any of you stubborn lot out there relate to this? Yep, thought so! I'd smashed my half marathon PB and gave talks at five schools in the previous week. I'm a motivational speaker, guys like us don't suffer from depression I'll have you know. Believe me when I say that I was trying my hardest to carry on with life as normal, but there was a part of me that still wanted answers. I still wanted to know what had happened '*that night*' in Fuerteventura.

It was December and we were in Lanzarote. I stood in a toilet cubicle and stared down at the toilet. Armitage Shanks... Hmm! Next to the toilet was a small sink unit. Suddenly my thoughts were interrupted as the door handle rattled, someone was waiting to use the cubicle. Turning my body, I was trying to work out if I was to slip over, would I fall straight down and bang my head on the sink? Nope, not physically possible, the science wouldn't allow it. What the hell happened? How did my life change in one of these toilet cubicles? The door rattled again, it was either the same person getting impatient or someone else needing to use the conveniences. I guessed they weren't going to perform some kind of reconstruction of a freak event from over three years ago.

I flushed the toilet, washed my hands and made my way back to the bar where Jules was sitting. Back to real life. She asked me what I'd been doing and why I'd been gone so long but I changed the subject quickly. I didn't want to admit that my toilet visits regularly became a crime scene investigation, trying to work out what the hell happened in that little tapas bar.

It was a couple of weeks before Christmas 2015 and here we were relaxing in shorts and t-shirts. A week in Lanzarote was the perfect place to run my 15th half-marathon of the challenge and have a bit of chill out time after our busy year. November had been full on and it included a whole week in a really tough school where discipline was a problem. I felt totally drained mentally and this break was exactly what we needed.

Jules had finished her Herceptin treatment and had started to feel small signs of recovery from the side-effects. I was buzzing physically from my challenge, but I felt probably the most emotional I've ever felt. You know that moment when you just want to cry but you have no idea why? Then you try and force some tears, but nothing comes out? Oh well, if it's not meant to be then time to carry on.

Normally we're off here, there and everywhere, but we spent most days of this trip just sitting by the pool. The hotel we were staying at was lovely and this was the downtime we needed. It had now been a year since Jules finished her chemo and she had a lovely, cute short hairstyle. We were reflecting on things one day as we sat in the sun, sipping a cocktail.

Suddenly it occurred to me how much I'd been pushing myself to try and get life back to how it was before all this happened to us. The doctor and neurologist had made some suggestions that I'd been dismissing, but perhaps they were right. I knew Jules was right because she was still suggesting that I stop ignoring all of these issues and start listening to my body and my mind. Trouble is, my mind was struggling to make sense of everything, even the simple things.

Jules was having a siesta on the sun lounger, so I went on my phone, looked on the Headway website and read the page entitled '*The Effects of Brain Injury*.' The first paragraph read:

"Even after a minor head injury, brain function can be temporarily impaired, and this is sometimes referred to as concussion. This can lead to difficulties such as headaches, dizziness, fatigue, depression, irritability and memory problems."

OK, my head injury was anything but minor and perhaps I'm the 0.01% who survived. So why am I experiencing some of the above? It continued:

"While most people are symptom-free within two weeks, some can experience problems for months or even years after a minor head injury."

Hmm, it still referred to a minor injury. I suppose the effects may apply to major brain injuries though. Let's keep reading:

"The more severe the brain injury, the more pronounced the long-term effects are likely to be. Survivors of more severe brain injury are likely to have complex long-term problems affecting their personality, their relationships and their ability to lead an independent life."

Well I'm happily married and running my own businesses, so relationships are fine. I'm independent but I suppose I'm a bit quieter than I was before. What else have you got on your website?

"Even with good rehabilitation, support and help in the community, survivors and their families are likely to face uncertain and challenging futures."

Confused! Yep, serious head injury, miracle survivor who can live life as normal. I'd been signed off from the hospital numerous times and was doing most of the stuff I did before my brain injury occurred. Perhaps it was the fact that I'd just been through the trauma of my wife being diagnosed with cancer and then having a journey of horrible treatment. Anyone is going to be stressed about that, surely? I'd had no community support and my future didn't seem uncertain.

I'm a man. I've been pushing the businesses and keeping myself fit whilst doing my absolute best for Jules, my family and friends. Where do I go from here?

By the time Jules woke up, I'd made a whole list of things in the notes section on my phone. The list described everything I felt I was experiencing including lack of focus, difficulty processing information, short-term memory loss, feeling snappy if challenged, feeling foggy, struggling with lots of background noise and feeling anxious for no apparent reason. The weirdest one was blanks in conversations, and then there was my complete obsession with the toilet crime scene investigations. It was also apparent that I wasn't enjoying some of the school sessions as much as usual and there seemed to be fewer of them. Jules looked relieved as I shared my list and added that I seemed to be obsessing over little things too. It felt good to be honest and I could see that perhaps Headway would help me to get over some of these issues. I'll give them a call in the New Year.

The following day I ran the Lanzarote Half Marathon and the 15 races in 2015 were complete. Crossing the finish line in Costa Teguise, Jules was standing there looking proud with her arms out waiting for a big, sweaty hug. After a quick change, I ate the biggest pizza I could find and we headed to a bar to enjoy a few pints in the sun as the football results came through. My team Northampton won 4-3 in an epic game at Luton to go top of the league to add a little bonus to the day.

As some of our 2015 goals had been achieved it was time to look ahead to 2016, onwards and upwards! Or was it all about to go downhill?

Chapter 17: Jules

2016 was an incredible year for lots of reasons. To help put this story together we dug out our old diaries and, on looking at what we somehow managed to achieve, this year looked crazy!

It was a year full of some more wonderful holidays and travels, going to see some great bands and we saw Mark's sister get married. I worked hard on our home-based business, growing that nicely along with Mark's support. Mark was successful in being appointed a company facilitator for our home-based business, which really gave him a boost in confidence! We spent weekends up in Darlington enjoying being grandparents visiting Isaac, and days at home with Thea.

A great moment came in the spring, when Mark came downstairs, and I immediately did one of my silly dances and twirls that I do when I'm happy and in a daft mood and declared, "I'm back, I'm back!"

It's so hard to explain exactly what I felt, other than a cloudiness had lifted and the feeling of having less of the normal energy that I was used to had disappeared. The drugs must have been out of my system and oh my goodness, that felt good! I could think more clearly, I felt internally alive and well and I just wanted to dance!

As is the norm nowadays we posted all of these amazing things on social media and friends were constantly telling us, '*Gosh, you're always so busy, here and there and having lots fun, wish I had your life.*'

Well you know that saying, '*You don't know what goes on behind closed doors*'? Nothing could be truer, as behind the scenes, things were going from bad to worse.

Mark's forgetfulness was causing problems; it seemed that 70% of our conversations he couldn't recall. He was still pushing himself and the fatigue was really kicking in. He was using all his energy to get through the school sessions and then just crashing with what we now know as mental exhaustion. Trying to have any kind of conversation about the situation was becoming more difficult than before. I could no longer say what I was really feeling or explain to him his behaviour. He would instantly bite back at me if I said anything that had even the tiniest hint of negativity to it. He would then go silent, for what seemed like hours, and hide behind his laptop if we were at home. If I ever tried to mention that he shouldn't be having so much '*screen*' time, then again, he would snap at me that he had to do what he was doing. If I questioned him as to what he was doing, he would try and fob me off with an excuse. It seemed he was happy '*tapping*' as I used to call it.

I could see the school work was bothering him; he was always uptight and worried constantly that he wasn't getting the bookings like he used to. He'd managed to deliver the wrong session at a school too which caused him great anxiety. He'd spend hours sifting through his records to confirm his suspicions. I know he talked quite often to other presenters and staff, but nothing that was said to him would ease his worried mind.

The company had also been in touch, concerned that his delivery wasn't up to scratch and gave him some negative feedback. All of this just added to his now quite low self-esteem. He'd attended a few meetings with them over the year and was keen to try to improve and add to the workshops they could offer, but it seemed it fell on deaf ears. Again, all this just made him frustrated.

Daniel, Russell, Roxanne and Lou were also asking me questions, '*Is Mark ok, he doesn't seem himself?*' or '*What's up with Mark? He seems very quiet and withdrawn!*' I explained a little of what was going on, but I was still quite confused with some of it to be honest.

I still couldn't get my head around the fact that one day we'd be somewhere where there was some background noise and he'd be perfectly ok, then a few days later it would be the worst thing ever and we'd have to leave immediately. Some days I could talk a little to him, and others it was a no-go area. Sometimes the changes happened throughout the day, and other days I could see straight away from the moment he woke up that things weren't going to plan in his head.

I'd try my best to listen and understand when he told me what he'd researched about what could be happening to him and how we could deal with it. However, when it seemed so erratic, it was hard to deal with and my happy dances in the kitchen quickly vanished.

December came and we received a message from the company that booked Mark saying that they required a Skype call with him. I instinctively knew what the outcome of this was going to be, I'd sensed it for some time. Mark was half the person he was. I've watched him present in schools and I used to cry each time with pride and laughter, he was amazing! But I figured a lot of that wasn't happening as much as it should.

Yes, I was right, they no longer want to use his services, gutted, god he didn't need this right now. His confidence was getting lower and this was just a huge kick in the stomach for him. He looked shocked and scared after he'd put the phone down and I could see he was trying to make some sense of it. It took hours of talking and going over all they had said to him, but there was no going back. I felt sooo bad for him, I knew he felt that he'd let me down and it was hard to know the right thing to say to make him feel better. I just hugged him loads and listened to him pour out some of his anger and frustrations with them.

I said, "Maybe this isn't such a bad thing you know. Maybe it's the kick up the bum we need? We can do it alone, just you and I, MAD4Life will be our full-time business. We've got lots of contacts, loads of resources and you always wanted to add more into what you deliver, so let's do this together. I'll start coming to all the sessions and learn them. We'll sort out the different jobs for each other within the business. What do you think?"

He hugged me and agreed this was the way forward. I'm so pleased he agreed but, blimey, I was really scared and nervous too. For too long we'd relied upon their bookings and to go solo now was hugely daunting. I didn't have any doubts in his ability to deliver outstanding workshops, it was whether we could get enough to cover the loss of income that we had just been served with. It was plain to see Mark was feeling even worse than me. His confidence had just been dealt a huge blow, but I knew we could make it work.

We'd booked flights down to Malaysia and Thailand, travelling on New Year's Eve for a month and as ever, we had a fabulous time exploring. We used this time to contact all the schools Mark had worked with and told them we'd gone out on our own, and bookings started coming in! They say that when one door closes, another one opens; well we were stepping through that door and we were going to give it all we'd got!

Chapter 18: Mark

"Are you OK babe?" Jules asked me.

Sitting on the sofa in the conservatory, I felt numb. I'd no longer be freelancing with the company I'd spent seven years in partnership with. I was angry and confused. So, after driving some stupid journeys all over the country and going above and beyond at times, it was now over. For what? It felt as if I'd just been dumped.

The last year had been a bit of a struggle. In March, we hit the busiest school period and I went to a school in Stratford. One of my colleagues had called the week before to say he had some negative feedback that he wanted to discuss with me. We were both presenting sessions at the same school so he said he'd talk to me about it there. I then spent the next week worrying about it of course.

Apparently three schools from the previous November had commented that my sessions weren't as expected. It didn't make sense. One school had actually written really good feedback on a report but then had asked for a full refund of the booking fee. It was as if someone was making something up. Another school had raved about the session on the day. The headmaster and deputy head had kept me talking for so long after a parent session, that I actually missed my train. The third school was lovely, but the lady there had felt that I simply wasn't on my game that day. Her comments were really encouraging, but I didn't know what to think.

Feeling a little stunned, we put together a plan. I suggested that a couple of my colleagues come and observe me in school and be honest on my delivery. This was arranged and my feedback was outstanding. The company had arranged an annual summer get-together and I joked asking if I was still on amber watch and in my probation period. The reply from the guys in the office was that everything was fine and just to go out there and smash it.

Great, I'll do just that!

The company had asked us, as fellow presenters, to arrange some training and development sessions over the summer holidays. This was to create some new programmes and redevelop their existing material. We were the creators and they were the sales guys. It was good fun but when you put eight creative people together, egos can sometimes fly. I felt that we were creating many off-the-shelf programmes that were too similar, but we went with the majority. I began to feel as if I was speaking out a little too much so reigned in my thoughts ahead of the new academic year.

Planning my first week back in school, I was really nervous. In fact, I hadn't felt like this since I first began presenting to big groups on my own. Back then it was excited and energetic nerves, but this time it was different.

Do you ever find that when you're scared of making a mistake, you actually end up making it? Well on day one, I went to a school in Cheshire and delivered completely the wrong programme! The students had a great day but no matter how many times I went back over the facts, it definitely said to deliver a workshop on Goals and not Study on the email. It seemed strange; the teacher didn't mention it on the day and commented what a great session it was. However, it was my mistake and time to take responsibility. Immediately I contacted the school and apologised hugely. An offer of a free session and I'd even pay my own train fare to make up for it.

Ok, we make mistakes, time to get back on it and smash it! The next few weeks were amazing. Great sessions, great feedback and a real buzz in the room. Things didn't feel right though. I was arriving at a school a bag of nerves, pulling off a great session and then running for the train to get home as quickly as I could. I couldn't work out what was happening. There was such a rush of adrenaline but it was totally wiping me out.

That was it! The dreaded call came through just before December and I was told we wouldn't be working together anymore. It didn't make sense at all. The issue was still around some negative feedback and, when I asked for details, it appeared to be from the same timeframe which was now well over a year ago.

I looked at Jules and she gave me a huge hug, you know, one that goes on forever! It was the best! The only person I needed right now was right there.

We took a few moments and she said to look at the positives. That year I'd been selected to be a company trainer for the network-marking company we worked with. Also, a local organisation had given us funding to deliver school sessions in Northamptonshire for the next two years. I couldn't be that bad at training and speaking, could I?

It was time to move on and move forward. We were just about to take a month off and travel around South-East Asia, so let's go and have some fun and come back and take advantage of new opportunities. The Chinese use the same word for crisis and opportunity so why not us?

Ok, so you may be wondering what happened with the charity, Headway? You may be questioning how come a year later, you're saying the same thing as you did in Lanzarote? Why have you not moved forward?

Well if we rewind a bit, I'll tell you. In the New Year I called Headway and explained my situation. I'd met some of the staff a few times before at different events and they were really lovely. After a good long chat, I got a similar response from them as I'd had from the neurologist. Now Headway are a charity and their funding had been reduced over the past few years, so I needed a solid referral in order for them to get funding to help me. Guess what? The able-bodied, fit, active guy who runs two businesses and runs marathons, didn't really fit the criteria. And that was cool, in my mind it just strengthened to me that I was OK. It was back to the attitude of, '*Oh, I'll be fine, I don't need any help*', as I thought, '*This will pass.*' All I wanted was to get my life back to normal, was that too much to ask for?

Chapter 19: Jules

Things were looking up, once we returned from travelling in February 2017. A lovely lady, whom Mark had worked with in the past, had been in contact before Christmas. She'd given us a contract to deliver numerous motivational assemblies in local schools. That gave us a springboard to start building up MAD4Life and we were so very grateful to her for this. Mark had certainly got his buzz back for delivering the sessions and especially now we had complete control of them. We could tailor the content to suit the schools which he wasn't allowed to do before. We were both creative and passionate about including more personal development teaching within them. It was great to see him enjoying the workshops.

A couple of months later, we had a call from a company using some government funding, who'd been recommended to use Mark to deliver motivational workshops in schools. They came and observed a session and took us on, amazing! They started booking us into their schools up in Lincolnshire and our business really started to take off for us. I did all the driving back and forth so Mark could save his energy and concentration. To start with I would just observe the sessions and make notes of where I thought we could change or improve them, but gradually I started taking part in them. This was something way out of my comfort zone, standing in front of 200+ students and presenting! I felt a fraud and nowhere near as good as Mark but eventually I really started to enjoy it.

I bet you're thinking by reading this that all seems fine now, but nothing could be further from the truth.

Mark had decided, when we got back in February, to go along to the Headway drop-in sessions as suggested over a year ago by his consultant. I went along to the first few sessions with him as I wanted so much for this to help us and for him find his way through this. They do such amazing work for people who've suffered terrible head injuries like Mark, but most of them hadn't been as lucky as him and were barely able to function. I didn't feel that they were making any difference other than to confirm that what we were experiencing was natural and to just expect and put up with it. I felt that it was actually making him worse, thinking this was it and there was no way out. I stopped attending as I believed it was actually having a negative impact on him, although he continued until the programme ceased.

I could see the rejection he'd had from his work in December had hit him really hard and now sleep was becoming very difficult for him. I'd spend nights listening to him fall asleep only to wake up moments later in sheer terror and fear. He could never remember what the dreams were, if there were any, or what they were about, but he would be shaking and scared as hell.

Our relationship was starting to really suffer too. We would try and go for a drink in the local pub but invariably it would end up that we couldn't speak to each other. Many nights he would come home and spend hours being sick and just hugging the toilet. I could do nothing to console him.

He'd say he didn't think I loved him anymore although I'd tell him every night that I did. I'd tell him, '*Nothing has changed, I still love you and I will always love you*'. I did and still do. I love him not just because he's my husband, but because I know the man that that made me fall in love him is still in there, I just wanted that man back so badly. I couldn't stand the pain that he and I were in. We'd gone from being the most loving, caring, free-spirited couple, to a couple that on a good day could just about hold a decent conversation. Gone were the days of spontaneously going out for the day, evening, or weekend. We couldn't do anything without it being planned in advance but more often than not Mark would bail at the last moment. He couldn't face being with people or was in such a dark place it wasn't worth even trying to go out and socialise.

This was particularly hard because I saw him being able to pick himself up and deliver some great workshops and have a whole school year group in the palms of his hands. They'd be listening to his every word and then straight afterwards, boom, down he went, and there was no making contact with him. I felt I'd lost him and wasn't sure of how to get him back. I think I was grieving for the life we used to have.

I started to think that actually it was just me imagining all this and maybe I'd got it all wrong. Perhaps I was just making it up. I know that at times I'd said the wrong thing to him and used to beat myself up for not understanding and thought I should take his backlashes. I could see he was struggling but at times it hurt so badly that I felt I had to say what I was feeling. I remember sitting in the local pub one night and saying, 'Do you know, I'm not sure I can go on like this.' I was really hoping that this might shock him into looking at where we were and make the changes needed. But it had the opposite effect and he cried himself to sleep while all I could do was just listen to him and cry silently myself.

I was tired; actually, I was exhausted. I'd been doing everything I could to make his life as easy as possible. All the driving and delivering the sessions plus all the admin and social media work was taking its toll on me and I was losing patience with him. Everything we did was centred around him, how he felt and making sure he was alright. There seemed no room for me or how I was feeling. This caused a lot of heartache between us and many horrible conversations and tears which only exasperated the situation.

Daniel, my eldest son, had to move in with us temporarily due to personal reasons in the middle of this year, 2017, and it wasn't long before he said,

"Mum, why haven't you told me how bad Mark is?"

"What do you mean?" I replied.

Daniel then told me that he felt Mark was in really bad place. He worked in care and knew what anxiety and depression looked like and how it can manifest itself. He told me that was where Mark was. I didn't know what to do for a moment; here was someone telling me what I think I mostly knew. Relief swept through me that I wasn't going mad, this really was happening and maybe, just maybe, it wasn't entirely my fault. I hugged him and cried and thanked him. It was a godsend for me having Daniel there and someone I could talk to. He understood what was happening and kept saying we needed to try and get proper help for Mark. However, any talk of this with Mark just fell on deaf ears.

Mid-October we went to the pub for a drink and to watch my beloved Manchester United play Benfica. Mark said he was going to message his sister and I said,

"Make sure you ask her if she's around on Tuesday when we're in London to catch up."

Twenty minutes later I asked, "What did she say?"

He replied "She's ok!"

"No, I meant is she around on Tuesday, I thought that's what you were going to find out?"

That was it, as simple as that. He went immediately downhill and into a complete shell of depression. That was all it was taking. He couldn't sleep again that night, tossing and turning and waking up almost screaming.

The next day we were due to drive up to Darlington and, on waking, I asked if he was ok and still wanted to go to which he replied '*yes*.' The journey was just awful; he was as white as a sheet and unable to hold a conversation. We only got as far as Leicester from Northampton and we had to stop at the services where he was really ill in the toilets. I asked if he wanted to go home but he didn't want to. He slept the rest of the way up there and on arriving just headed upstairs to bed.

Roxanne and I took Isaac out and she asked what the hell was going on. I broke down and let it all out. She was just wonderful and listened to all I had to say. Being a psychiatric nurse specialising in teenage problems she confirmed he had bad anxiety and depression and really needed to seek urgent help.

The next day Mark and I looked after Isaac while Roxanne went to work. He was coming up for two years old and had that wonderful, innocent way of taking everything bad away. We had great fun with him. We had to drive back home on Friday evening due to commitments over the weekend. I decided to seize my chance of having us both trapped in car for at least three hours to talk.

It went ok-ish and Mark was fairly receptive. My whole point to him was that neither of us could continue like we were. I told him of my conversation with Roxanne and what her thoughts were, but the main thing I wanted to stress to him was that we needed help. Not just him but us, we were in this together. I was acutely aware by this time that he felt he was alone with this. He blamed himself for everything and thought that I didn't love him. I wanted so desperately for him to understand, no matter what, I'm with him, I love him, but we just needed to go to the doctors and find out where we can get some help. I felt we made some progress, he started to open up and talk a little more freely about how he was feeling. It felt good to hear and as I was driving, I let him talk. He agreed that we needed to seek help and that we would go to the doctors. Hooray! I'm not for one minute thinking that one appointment and all would be fixed but finally, it felt like we might be getting somewhere.

Chapter 20: Mark

Yay, the day arrived. It was 27th February 2017 and I walked through the door of Headway for the first time. A leaflet was handed to me that read, '*Headway are pleased to announce a new specialist brain injury monthly drop-in pilot*.'

At first, it was a little nerve-wracking. I was armed with my long list of side-effects in the notes section on my phone that I'd revisited and updated. Feeling a little like a hypochondriac who was going to see a psychiatrist, it felt a bit made up. Having been discharged from everywhere I'd visited so far, I half expected to be told to go away and get on with things. It was actually the opposite.

A member of staff gave me a guided tour before we sat on a sofa and chatted. It felt incredibly relaxed and welcoming. Another member of staff joined us, and I was reassured that most of the things I was experiencing were quite common following a brain injury. This was incredibly helpful just to offload a little.

I asked Jules to come along to the next session. Again, we all sat on the same sofa and just chatted. After leaving, Jules asked me a question.

"What exactly is this doing for you?"

Other than saying everyone was really nice and it was good to share, I was a little puzzled. She then pointed out to me that I was more stressed than ever and seemed more in my shell than before. She was right!

Since returning from a month of travelling around Malaysia and Thailand in January, I felt like a bag of nerves. Our backpacking adventure was magical; we visited some incredible places and met some amazing people. Neither of us wanted to come home, naturally, but we were excited about having total control of our businesses now and the freedom to take whatever direction we wanted. However, my confidence was at rock bottom. Now I was turning up to a school and feeling incredibly anxious. The negative feedback issue was still in the back of my mind. What if I wasn't good enough?

After a couple of months trying to make sense of it all, nothing seemed to add up. I'd been in touch with the company I'd been partnered with again and been given so many conflicting stories, it was a minefield. There weren't any specific examples of exactly which school had said what, other than the original feedback given over a year ago. I'd then wake up in the night and ponder why? Perhaps it was because I was travelling by train and a little less flexible? Perhaps my anxiety had been affecting my performance? Maybe I'd spoken out a couple of times about some ideas instead of following the status quo? Was this brain injury fatigue just getting boring for them and it was easier to let me go? Sadly, no matter how many questions I asked myself there were still no answers. Now I always think there are two sides to an outcome, so I never for one minute wanted to say it was their fault or mine. I just wanted to move on but I couldn't.

Despite this feeling, everywhere we went, the schools loved us. We also got a call one day from an organisation in Lincolnshire. They had been given my number by the University of Northampton who recommended me highly. Wow, I was pleasantly stunned. It was a real honour to be spoken so highly of.

I'd also been getting really stuck into my training with the network-marketing company and getting rave feedback there. I got regular comments such as, '*This was the best training I've attended,*' from delegates and '*Mark is the most laid back and fun trainer I've trained alongside,*' from fellow trainers. Even the training managers and the company's network director were impressed. I'd walk out of every session absolutely buzzing. Trouble is, I'd then go into an anxiety-frenzy, scared that perhaps I would get found out. Maybe I'm not that good and my weakness would show through and everything would come crashing down? Of course, it didn't though. We were visiting schools and the rave reviews continued.

I carried on visiting Headway every month and loved chatting to the staff and volunteers there. Although there was no real set agenda to the visits, I was constantly reassured that everything I was experiencing was consistent with a brain injury. However, on one particular visit my view changed a little.

I'd been invited to an open day put on by patients and the place was absolutely packed. On the drop-in days, it was normally only me and staff there, as the pilot scheme hadn't had such a great take up. I met some incredibly humbling people. I met a young girl who'd fallen while rock climbing. She now struggled to spend more than three hours awake and walked with a stick. I chatted to the young girl's parents and they told the story of how she had to drop out of university but is now volunteering to teach painting for Headway. I went into my positive motivation mode and called out to her to keep setting her goals in her recovery. Another guy had suffered a stroke and was in a wheelchair. Everyone in the room was physically disabled following their brain injury. As we chatted sitting on that sofa, I suddenly felt like a huge fraud. Yep, the business owner and runner who had just spent a month backpacking had no right to be here. These guys needed Headway much more than me. I didn't say anything to the staff, but something didn't feel right.

I carried on attending the monthly drop-in sessions but sadly Headway were still desperately short of funds and the pilot hadn't worked as well as they'd expected. In fact, only one other person had attended regularly, and I'd only actually met them once. After a year of the pilot scheme, I was told that unfortunately they wouldn't be able to continue with the drop-in sessions, but I was welcome to pop in for a chat if I wanted to. I felt quite deflated because another year had passed, I'd finally reached out for support but felt as if I was still stuck in the same place. Five years on and I'd have to deal with it myself I suppose, but it wasn't getting any easier.

Daniel had moved in with us for a while and our granddaughter Thea visited regularly which was lovely. Jules kept telling me how she'd noticed how stressed I was and how I would snap at the smallest things. Then my mum started asking Jules, '*What's wrong with Mark?*'

Although everything was buzzing with our businesses, I still felt awful. I'd have nights where I couldn't sleep and then have to either push through the following day or go and lie down for a couple of hours. Panic attacks became more regular. I felt alone, who could I talk to? Jules now had Dan at home, but I felt that I was letting everyone down or annoying them. The cycle would go from high to low to high and then crash. It would be anxiety before a school visit, push, push, push, then perform. This would be a real buzz and the great feedback would follow. There's the high! Next... boom! Tired! Fatigue! Time to sleep followed by waking up feeling a complete let-down because I'd wasted time. Now the low point... feeling irritable and alone! That was the cycle.

Down, low and fragile, that's how I felt! Add that to the feeling of being alone and having nobody to reach out to. It was affecting everything in my life, every single day. The littlest comment or slightest knockback and, bang, I was floored. I'd go back into my shell and want to hide away from the world. What the hell happened to me?

Jules is the closest person to me in life. We live together, work together, holiday together and, most of all, have the strongest love for each other that is worth more than anything on this planet. Trouble is, I felt that I was a terrible person to be around. In my head I felt that I was letting my wife down every single day. I felt like I was making her miserable and I didn't know what to do about it.

This would be that very cycle. Jules would notice I was struggling and perhaps not understand why. I mean, I didn't understand what was going on so I couldn't expect her to. I'd go into my shell and end up snapping at any suggestions or criticism. This would frustrate Jules who in turn would snap back. I became scared to say anything because I didn't want to cause any more hurt or pain. This of course resulted in higher anxiety and lower confidence.

In fact, everything was loaded with anxiety: being around people, being on my own, delivering a training session or being at home. Apart from when I was travelling or running, I felt trapped in my own world of never-ending darkness.

Chapter 21: Jules

The following weeks were pretty hectic with school bookings, visits down to Mark's dad, Katy and Ethan, Thea and Isaac's birthdays etc. and by the time we came to board our flight to Goa for a month on 24th November, no call to the doctors had been made. However, there was a slight improvement in his overall demeanour since our long talk so I decided we would try and carry on these long talks and get him to open up while we're sitting on those lovely relaxing beaches.

I remember being on the flight to India and suddenly thinking, '*Shit, we've never been here before, we're going for a whole month, what if we don't like it? What if we don't get on with the people and the culture? Maybe we've made a big mistake?*'

Absolutely not, Goa was wonderful; we started in the north and worked our way down to the south.

Arriving and going through customs took a while, we were tired, and it was late. We got a taxi to where we'd planned to stay for the first two nights; it really was the middle of the night their time and the place seemed all shut up. Thankfully our taxi driver phoned and managed to wake them. We had a lovely long rest and then headed into the small town where we were staying for some breakfast. This probably wasn't the nicest of places, but we were heading up north the following day.

By teatime we were sat on the beach watching the locals enjoying themselves when Mark exclaimed, '*Jules look at this message from Aunty Annette.*' It had come through as we'd arrived at the airport but with the chaos, he'd missed it.

Mark's dad had had a massive stroke and they were trying to get hold of us as it was uncertain if he was going to make it through the night! Shit! We hastily grabbed all our things and ran to the nearest restaurant. I asked them if they have Wi-Fi, told them I needed really good Wi-Fi and we called Katy. We were both shaking and holding hands at this point, not knowing what we were going to hear.

Thankfully he had survived the night and although still very poorly was stabilising. '*Right, we'll get the next flight home*' I told her, but she talked us out of it and said to hang fire for the moment. It was really hard doing that. Mark was clearly very upset and worried. The next morning, we got a taxi up to the north of Goa where we'd planned to stay for four nights. Mark's dad was continuing to do well, so we decided to stay. Thank god for Facetime and WhatsApp, that's all I can say. Aunty Annette was brilliant.We'd message and talk every few hours and she'd tell us the whole truth in her wonderful no holds barred way!

We stayed the whole month as planned and half-way through there was the Goa River Marathon. Mark completed the Half Marathon and I did the 10k race. It started really early in the morning due to the heat. I was really worried as I'm not really a runner and don't enjoy full blown races, however, I totally loved this experience, especially coming 10th in my age category. Sounds great hey, but I'll be honest, there were only 20 of us in that age group! Mark didn't have his best run, but didn't beat himself up too much thankfully.

We headed down south after the race and found a little bit of heaven on earth. A gorgeous little village called Patnem with stunning beaches, a few restaurants and shops and it was just the most relaxing place ever.

We'd spent a lot of the days when we were relaxing on the beach writing our first book to go with our school workshops. I was reading The Chimp Paradox and using this to help with Mark and our book and this was really helping us to talk about Mark's anxiety and how we can deal with this on our return home.

It was also the holiday where we found out that Russell and Roxanne were expecting twins, double trouble and double the excitement!

It truly was the hardest place we'd ever had to leave, neither of us wanted to come home. We'd relaxed, the places we'd visited were so beautiful, the people were incredibly friendly and the food, oh the food, it was just to die for. Why would we want to come home?

We arrived home though on 23rd December, just in time for Christmas. Daniel had decorated the house and bought some supplies in for us and yes it was great to see him and be home for all the Christmas excitement and see our family. We went up north to celebrate New Year and congratulate Russell and Roxanne on the impending twins. Bless them, they were really excited but nervous too, having twins when you already have a very energetic two and half year old is somewhat daunting. A scan later on showed the twins were both boys, think they're starting to create their own football team!

I was all excited once we got back home, thinking of all the plans we'd made whilst in Goa. One of them was that we were going to complete two, yes two, marathons that year! It had always been on my bucket list to complete this distance just once and I wanted it to be the Beachy Head Marathon in Eastbourne. However, Mark also talked me into doing one in London in April 2018 that his running club had organised. What had I let myself in for?

It took less than a week into the new year of being home for Mark to morph back into the dark, distant, non-communicative, hard to reach man he'd been before we went way. I couldn't believe it; I really couldn't believe it. I thought we'd made some headway over the past couple of months and especially whilst away but obviously not, gutted! I just remember one morning in early January he was head down at the desk and I tried to ask him something and got no reply, he'd gone! My heart was breaking and I just picked up my keys and left the house. I had no idea where I went or what I did, but I couldn't stay. I felt at such a dead-end with nowhere to turn to. We'd tried hypnotherapy which he said really helped and gave him coping mechanisms to use when he felt the anxiety coming on or building. We'd also tried yoga and meditation (which really helped me). I'd ask him if was using these techniques to help calm his mind and would say '*yes*' but I never actually witnessed it.

So, there we were at the start of another year. 2018 promised to be a good one but we were no further forward with Mark. I started doing the training needed for the first marathon and, I'll be honest, I really enjoyed being out with my own thoughts. Many a time

I'd come back home and just think it's down to him now. I didn't know what else to do so just accepted that this was how our lives were going to be, we'd continue to bounce from great highs to very deep lows and that's it.

He was now caught in what I can only describe as a vicious cycle. For example, he would wake and feel good but by lunchtime he would start to burn out and lose any focus and concentration and would go to bed to rest. Quite often he would sleep for at least a good couple of hours but would still feel tired when he woke. This would frustrate the hell out of him and then he would spend the rest of the day beating himself up, feeling useless and that he'd achieved nothing except a horrible atmosphere in the house. Everything seemed to stress him out. If he was trying to type something on his phone all you would hear was him swearing at it and throwing it down in temper. If we were driving and the traffic light changed to red it would completely piss him off as if they'd changed just to annoy him.

His OCD was now out of control and, to be honest, driving me mad! For example, if he was putting together new slides for our school workshops and, maybe a full stop wasn't lined up or it looked the slightest bit out of sync, the irritation this would cause him along with the time he would take correcting it, was huge.

I'd say, "Do you know, I don't think anyone is going be looking at that, or will notice that maybe the word isn't exactly millimetre by millimetre in the centre." However, he'd persist until he felt it was perfect, even though it was causing him such annoyance!

The bad dreams or night terrors were now far more frequent. It was so pitiful lying next to him listening to him struggling with his emotions. Constantly waking in sheer horror, shaking or sometimes crying. The anxiety had gotten a real hold of him and this awful cycle, which we didn't know how to break, just made him more and more depressed. Often, if he'd had a really bad day, his stomach would be in such knots that he'd spend hours hugging the toilet being sick. I lost count of the times I had to wake him curled up on the floor of the bathroom.

From everything we'd read up on, I came to just accept that this is him now, this is where we were. I'd just try to help him get through these bad times, as best as I possibly could, by trying not to react or get annoyed with him, and just help take away some of his obstacles. This was quite hard! Sometimes I was tired and fed up with it all and would say something that, looking back, wasn't the most helpful, but I couldn't help it. For me, it was the fact that every day was so inconsistent, the drops in moods weren't always the same and what was ok one day wouldn't be the next.

Don't get me wrong, we had some fabulous times this year as well. We both completed the marathon down in London. It was a great experience for me, quite hard and a bit soul destroying. The route was going up and down the same tow path next to the Thames eight times. By the sixth time, trust me, you hated the path, the bridge you had to go over and the pub you went past with families enjoying a beer and food! So many of Mark's running club stayed until I finished to cheer me through my last lap; they're truly an amazing group of people!

We had some fantastic sessions in wonderful schools and met some inspirational teens and teachers. Throughout this entire ordeal this is one thing that really brought us together: the passion to make a difference and help teenagers to be the best they can be. I think this managed to keep us going through the dark times.

We enjoyed some great holidays including a short one to Majorca where Mark completed a half marathon and I did the 10k. I totally enjoyed it and we were both buzzing afterwards.

In June I went up to look after Isaac while Roxanne and Russell delivered us the most beautiful, adorable, cutest twin boys I've ever seen; they're amazing and I'm the proudest nanny in the whole world!

Chapter 22: Mark

Being addicted to travel, we booked another backpacking adventure to India to end the year. It was fabulous. We had such an amazing adventure again, this time navigating the state of Goa before coming home just in time for a lovely Christmas. Whilst away, we laughed, relaxed, had adventures and loved every minute. Reflecting on the year past, we felt free from the ties of anything. I was myself again, my anxiety seemed to drop dramatically, it was amazing. We entered and ran in the Goa Marathon Festival whilst there. Other than an occasional wobble, the month we spent there was magical. We chatted and I felt clear in my mind that all would be good when we got back. Being away, I felt I'd discovered myself again and I could do it. My confidence could and would soon return.

I came home with good intentions but a few days after Christmas and, bang, it was back to square one! I felt broken and couldn't explain why. Could we just get back on a plane and go back to India? Perhaps I needed to escape life in England! Maybe we should tour the world and run! They seemed to be the only two things I could do without falling to pieces. Why was everything falling apart again, and how could I put it back together?

While we were in Goa, we set some goals and entered two marathons in 2018. Jules had never done this distance before, but it had been on her list for some time. We both trained for the April marathon in Walton-on-Thames and it was a brilliant experience. Around 40 members from my running club, Northampton Road Runners, took part in the small, low key event and we both did it. I was holding back the tears when Jules crossed the finish line to cheers from my running buddies.

That high was followed by another quick crash and within days, I was back to that scared bird who wanted to fly away. So we did! We made spring trips to Tenerife and Fuerteventura and had the most relaxed and wonderful weeks. This was the second time I'd visited Fuerteventura since my accident, but we stayed in the north again, well away from the scene of the crime.

So, two amazing and fun trips but then back home and... you guessed it... bang! Fragile, tired, anxious, down, low and scared. I'd lie on the bed at home in the afternoon and just dream of selling everything and moving away somewhere. It was strange, nobody around me was horrible, in fact they were all their usual lovely selves. We never made a habit of hanging around negative people anyway.

The highs and lows were spiking even more now as the year passed. One minute everything would be fine and we would be enjoying ourselves and then I'd be through the floor. We'd pop round the local pub for a cheeky drink while planning our week ahead and within an hour, I'd be standing in the toilet cubicle, physically shaking and screaming! These screams couldn't be heard by anyone because absolutely nothing would come out.

As the year passed, I still had no answers. We did some really cool things and this relentless pattern would repeat. We booked more trips in the summer and autumn: another week in Fuerteventura (I'll tell you more about that later) and Majorca (we did the Palma 10K and half marathon there and it was brilliant).

Probably the most notable boom to bust for me was in September when we made a trip to Braemar to visit the Highland Games. It was such an exciting weekend.

Russell had coached the army tug of war team and taken them to the final at Braemar. They were favourites to win the gold medal in front of the Queen. Russ had also egged me on to compete in the fell race event. This was basically running to the top of a very big hill and back down again, finishing in the arena, packed with around 3,000 people. I didn't need much egging on to be honest!

We made the long journey with Warwick and picked Roxanne up from Darlington on the way. Staying in Dundee, I was really excited for the weekend. I did the fell race and we watched Russ win the gold. What an amazing day and it was time to celebrate. After a few drinks and some food, I suddenly found myself sitting on a bench alone by the River Tay. Nothing made sense. After an amazing day, I'd had to battle anxiety and then collapsed. Not physically but my whole brain simply shut off. It was awful! I felt I'd let everyone down and ruined what was a once in a lifetime memory. What the hell just happened?

Jules, Warwick and Roxanne headed into town to celebrate with Russell, but I slipped back off to the AirBnB because I knew it would be quite busy and noisy in the pubs. Multiple noises in a busy place is horrendous when you've suffered a brain injury. Your whole senses are disorientated, and it sometimes feels as if the room is spinning.

As I laid on the bed in the room watching Match of the Day, I knew I'd made the right decision not to go. My anxiety was through the roof and I was physically shaking. Trouble is, I knew how awkward this made things for everyone else so the next morning I just played it down and didn't talk about it.

This pattern continued. I was trying my best to hold it together in public. Being a speaker, I had to. Do you hear those stories of pop stars who perform on stage and everyone thinks their life is great? Then behind the scenes you later learn that they've checked into rehab? Well I started feeling a bit rock and roll.

Actually, I wish it was as glamourous as it sounded but it wasn't. We were absolutely smashing it on stage in schools though. Jules had been co-delivering workshops with me and we were pulling off some amazing sessions. The brilliant feedback continued but then my brain would simply shut off afterwards and sometimes I'd barely be able to communicate with Jules on the drive home.

Proof was in the pudding though; we were obviously doing something right...

"And the winner of the Enterprising Business of the Year goes to... (open envelope) ... MAD4Life!"

Oh wow, that's us! We've won!

We finished runners up in the Business Innovation Award and we were bouncing off the ceiling after winning this accolade at the Northamptonshire SME Business Awards. Jules and I ran to the stage, hugging friends along the way. After posing for a couple of photos, we returned to the table and toasted with a glass of champagne. I knew we'd win, just knew it! There was an inner confidence inside me, the first time I'd felt that for ages. Fellow business owners flocked around us and offered congratulations and there were hugs from strangers. Weeks after the event, our email inbox and social media feeds were still full of congratulations.

Rock and roll indeed. Here's the Oscar or Emmy for the washed-up rock star who needed some rehab. As I said, it didn't feel that glam, but this was an ultimate high.

The day after picking up this award, we made a Friday morning journey down to Eastbourne to take part in the Beachy Head Marathon. We sort of floated all the way down there and checked into our hotel still buzzing.

Now if you've ever seen the London Marathon on telly or even run it before, you'll know what it's all about. The streets of the capital come alive with crowds lining the streets. The cheering is immense and there's fancy dress and landmarks everywhere. Well the Beachy Head Marathon is nothing like that. You either run up a hill or down one. There's one flat bit around mile 10 through a cute little village.

We did it! It was the hardest event I've ever done and I was so proud of Jules. She's not a lover of running but she'd now completed her second marathon of the year. We made our way into a pub and celebrated the past few days, winning an award and then completing a ridiculously hard marathon. Talk about a high moment to build on. That's it, I can do it. No more worrying, no more anxiety, I'm on top of the world. Let's stay here and keep flying high!

Chapter 23: Jules

The twins were just three weeks old and we took a holiday back to one of our favourite destinations, Fuerteventura. We had a late flight and when we got to the hotel, I tried to sleep. I had a nagging worry in my head after Russell had told me that Hugo, one of the twins, wasn't too good. Early the next morning I messaged him, as I couldn't shake my concern. He told me he'd worsened through the night and they were now in hospital. Hugo was on a drip being given antibiotics and having tests to find out what was wrong. I was beside myself with worry and just wanted to come home and get up to Darlington, if only to help them out.

Later that day Russell messaged to say they were going to take a lumbar puncture from Hugo and test for meningitis. I could sense from his messages the huge concern they were both feeling. The pictures they sent of our little grandson with a cannula in his tiny arm were just gut wrenching. We decided to go for a run along the beach path but I had to stop, as every time I thought of poor Hugo, my chest tightened and I couldn't breathe. We spent the rest of the day just walking, talking and praying that he was going to be alright and checking flights home. It wasn't until way after dinner that night that Russell was in a position to call and update us.

I sat in the hotel lobby, as it was the quietest area, to be told that they were testing and treating Hugo for viral meningitis and encephalitis.

"What the hell is that?"' I asked.

Russell tells me, "You don't want to know but pray that it's viral meningitis, that's his best option."

I sat there crying, broken hearted for them and what they're going through and that I wasn't there to help. I went back to the pool area to find Mark and told him the news through buckets of tears. People were watching obviously wondering what was going on. We went back to our apartment and sat on the balcony trying to understand what the hell had just happened. I googled encephalitis and boy did I pray for the other option. We just laid in bed that night staring at the ceiling, with my phone in hand in case they called again, and prayed and prayed for the little fella.

The praying worked. It was viral meningitis and the prognosis was that he should make a full recovery, thank the lord for that! We decided not to take the flight home after discussing it with Russell but one of things that we did do was go back and visit the restaurant where Mark had that fateful pee!

It wasn't something that we'd planned to do that holiday, but had decided to go to a particular beach that we love on the island. This meant driving through Costa Calma where we'd stayed in 2012. As we approached the resort I asked Mark, '*Shall we go and have a look round*?' to which he replied, '*yeah why not!*'

The hotel we'd stayed in was now empty and derelict, but you could gain access to the grounds. It was very eerie and run down. We found our apartment and wandered round to the pool area. It felt very strange and brought back all sorts of difficult memories and feelings. We walked down the road to the restaurant, but as it was only about 11am, it was closed so off we went to the beach as planned. However, Mark wanted to come back later and go inside to see if it would bring back any recollection of what had happened.

We returned later and walked in; it had changed a little but was mostly the same. Mark couldn't remember where we'd sat so I showed him. We ordered a beer for Mark and wine for me and began to recall that eventful evening. I felt all the emotions come flooding back and couldn't hold back the tears. I went around to the toilet where it happened and everything was still the same. Mark then went too and spent some time there to see if any memory returned, but nothing did. This was something he's often wondered about doing, in the hope that it would spark a memory and maybe give us the answers to what actually happened. The consultants back home had asked if he suffered from black-outs or fits but no, never and if he did that night it would have been the first. We're glad that we took this time to go back and visit the crime scene. Although it didn't give any real insight or clues as to what happened, we now knew it wouldn't. It helped put that idea to bed for good.

We were quite drained by the time we got back to our hotel. It had been a strange holiday, yes, it was beautiful, the weather was great, we had lots of nice runs and walks, but with all that had happened, it was very emotional.

Thankfully Hugo has made a full recovery and is now a most wonderful, happy, cheeky one year old that brings us all much happiness and joy along with his twin brother, Oscar.

I recall as a child seeing the Highland Games on the news and wondering what that was all about, but now I know. Russell got involved with his regiment's Army Tug of War team a couple of years ago and really loved it. The previous year they'd gotten to the finals up in Braemar, where the Highland Games are held, and won silver which was absolutely fabulous. This year he was now managing the team and they were having a sensational season; they were unbeaten in all competitions. All the Army's hopes were pinned on them winning the pinnacle of the season, Braemar! We arranged to go up and watch along with Warwick and set off to meet up with Roxanne in Darlington on the Thursday.

Friday morning came and we were all excited as we were then heading up to Dundee where we'd booked an AirBnB, but Mark didn't seem quite himself and was a bit distant. The drive up there was glorious, I'd never been to Scotland and was just taking it all in. That night we all went for a walk along the river and found a nice pub in the town for some food and drink. As you can imagine, on a Friday night in Scotland in a pub, it was fairly busy and immediately this put Mark into a panic and sent him to planet Mark. He looked, and I'm sure felt, really uncomfortable in a busy noisy place and I tried my best to find a quietish table for us to sit down and eat. He really didn't enjoy it and was very quiet and withdrawn. It made the whole night a little uncomfortable for me, Roxanne and Warwick as we tried in vain to carry on as normal.

The next day was so exciting! We'd picked up an ex-army friend of Russell's from the railway station and headed over the hills to Braemar. Mark had entered the fell race which looked bloody crazy but was in high spirits and eager to see what this hill looked like.

The place was just incredible. Much better than I'd ever imagined or remembered from the telly all those years ago and the weather was great too! It came time for Mark's race and off he went full of anticipation and excitement. He thoroughly enjoyed the whole experience and made it back down within the allotted time, amazing and bloody well done to him. Such an achievement.

The Tug of War combats began and Russell's team got through to the finals. We were ecstatic. It was time for the final and we managed to get a good spot and watched them win. It truly was one of the proudest mum moments of my life, we were all leaping up and down cheering and shouting Russell's name. He was then presented with the trophy from, none other than, Her Majesty the Queen. What a day and what a triumph for him!

After the games we drove back to Dundee and got changed. The plan was to grab some food and then head into Dundee Centre and meet up with Russell and the team. We found a lovely Indian restaurant and ordered food. Mark by this time was very quiet and I knew he hadn't enjoyed the drive back, sat in the back of the car. Warwick was driving and I was in the front navigating. Mark looked like a startled rabbit in the headlights every time I looked at him and I kept asking him if he was ok, to which he just nodded yes.

As our food came out and we were chatting about where we were going to meet Russell, Mark turned to me and said he didn't think he was going to come with us as he wasn't feeling up to it.

"I knew you were going to say that and that you wouldn't come and join in the celebrations" was my reply.

I understood his reasons, but he had totally slipped back into the scared, can't communicate mode. I'm aware this may sound a bit harsh, but I'll be honest, I was glad he wasn't coming. It meant I could go out and enjoy the evening without constantly having to worry about him and how he was feeling or coping. It goes without saying that I love him dearly, but have you ever gotten to a point in your life where you've nothing left to give? In that exact moment, that's where I was. I felt completely exhausted and craved some normality, just for one night. We got a taxi and off we went leaving Mark to walk back on his own. I could hardly kiss him. I was gutted he couldn't let himself relax and come and enjoy the celebrations, especially after his amazing feat of the day too.

We had a wonderful evening and it felt so good sitting in a pub with family and friends. There was lots of banter and laughter. I wasn't having to make sure Mark was alright or needing to leave early because he couldn't cope with the situation or surroundings. But this was our life now, we couldn't go out and be ourselves like we used to. Everything had to be planned around how Mark was feeling and where he felt he could sit in a pub or restaurant so it wasn't too noisy or crowded. If he wasn't in a good place mentally, either we didn't go, or if we did, we would invariably sit in silence.

Later that year Mark decided to enter us into the Northamptonshire SME Business Awards for our MAD4Life work in schools. We'd entered two categories: Enterprising Business of the Year and Innovative Business of the Year and got through to the finals in both. We were so excited! The evening of the finals was on the 25th October and off we went all dolled up, well almost! Mark never wears a tie and, although it was a black-tie event, he still wouldn't wear one!

The Innovation category was being announced and to our delight we came second, how amazing was that? Later they began to explain the Enterprising Business of the Year category. They announced third place, then second and began to describe the company who'd won. Mark turned to me and said '*That sounds like us*!' and guess what? It was!

We'd won, oh my god, I couldn't believe it. I was in shock, little us, our little business had won this prestigious award. We were beside ourselves with joy and amazement! We could hardly take it in. There we were, on stage, receiving the award to loud applause and cheers, whilst having our photos taken. It was just amazing! It took weeks for it to sink in. A little idea we'd had many, many years previously on a beach in Ibiza to start our own business and here we were winning this against some awesome competition!

Mark was on cloud nine, he was so happy, and I was delighted to see him like this. The following day we headed down to Eastbourne and completed the Beachy Head Marathon. I think our euphoria kept us going. It was really tough and after 20 miles we were still loving it. It was a cold but bright and windy day. Then we met the Seven Sisters, they all had names and I renamed the sixth one '*the bitch*', she was a tough hill. Those last few miles were the hardest ever and seemed to go on forever, but we did it and went straight to the pub around the corner from the finish line for a well-earned beer and rest.

We were still buzzing once we got home. More so for our upcoming month-long travels down to Kerala in Southern India and then onto Sri Lanka, a place we'd always wanted to visit. Things are finally looking up!

Chapter 24: Mark

Welcome to CSI from The Med! As I mentioned earlier, for a few years, my crime scene investigations in toilet cubicles had taken place all over the world. I'd still stand there and try and work out what the hell had happened. Just as I explained in Lanzarote, it didn't matter where I was, I would just wonder how this every day act changed my life. Medical experts advise that you're never going to remember what actually happened after losing consciousness in a traumatic head injury so don't bother trying. It doesn't stop you wondering though.

Well we bagged a last-minute deal to Fuerteventura again in the summer and stayed close to the centre point of the island, giving us a great base to explore. A few days in, we decided to drive south to Sotavento, a stunning beach where the surfing championships were taking place. This involved a journey past Costa Calma, the scene of the accident.

Since last visiting the south, a new bypass had been built in the south of the island meaning Costa Calma could be missed out. Good news if you want to avoid some painful (in more ways than one) memories. Moments later, we'd turned off the junction to Costa Calma and turned right at the roundabout into the area where the Hotel Althay Apartments stood.

We drove past the medical centre that cost a Euro to get to by taxi, past the little tapas bar and parked up outside the now-derelict hotel. Opening the car door, we wandered into the hotel complex. It was eerie! Paths had been overtaken by weeds and paint was flaking off the walls. Some bits had been covered in graffiti and old furniture was discarded outside rooms that had been locked for some time.

Jules retraced our steps back to our room, showing me various points where I wanted to stop and sleep on that fateful night. Surreal is an understatement to describe this moment. The place where time stood still for us had also frozen in its existence.

Next, we wandered towards the tapas bar which was closed until the evening. We peered through the window and Jules showed me where we'd sat that night. Nope, no memory came back!

We went back to the car and continued our journey south, visiting Jandia and then Sotavento. A few painful memories came back, but I felt incredibly calm. No anxiety, no panic but a niggle in the back of my mind. I'd come this far, surely this was the moment to take that final step. It was a sort of now-or-never moment. I wanted to re-open the investigation and carry out a thorough examination of the crime scene. I chatted to Jules as we sat on the beach and we decided to head back to the tapas bar when it opened and have a drink there. The intrigue was so high in my mind.

We drove back to Costa Calma and just after 5pm, we walked through the door of the tapas bar and the waiter showed us to a table. We ordered a couple of drinks and surveyed the layout. Jules painted the picture of that evening back in August 2012, showing me where the other couple dining sat and where a part of the bar used to be. She also needed to use the toilet so the inevitable first visit to behind the scenes was made. As Jules returned, she sat down and had a few tears. It was a pretty painful and surreal moment. Our drinks arrived and the friendly waiter made conversation. We dropped into the chat that we'd visited some years ago and he told us of a couple of changes that had been made to the bar recently but other than that, everything else remained the same. At that moment, I stood up and headed to the toilet.

This was it! I'd played this moment in my head over and over again, about making the short walk around the corner of the bar and into the cubicle where my life had changed forever. Does that not sound a bit weird? A life changing moment happened here in a toilet? Hmm, indeed!

Taking in a deep breath, I opened the door and walked inside. At the end of the small cubicle, there was a toilet on the right-hand side. Next to it was a sink and then the wall recessed to where the door was. I looked around. There was no window, so I was now 100%

certain that nobody jumped through the window, whacked me on the head and ran off. That wasn't a real theory anyway but at least it had been banished for sure. There was no low hanging ceiling or pipework and nothing to fall from above to take me out. That was also dismissed a long time ago because the impact of the blow to my head was to the side and consistent with a fall.

Next, it was time for the famous signature move that had been reconstructed thousands of times in various locations around the globe. I stood in front of the toilet and imagined falling sideways. This was it, this time it was real. I had the exact dimensions to work with. There was no hearsay as to what might have been to my right as I fell. No algebra or trigonometry was needed here, just simple bodily movements. Stand here, fall that way. Stand there, collapse here. After about five minutes my mind was clearer as to what had happened. Time to end the inquest and close the case. There were no witnesses and no CCTV footage (thankfully, as it's a toilet cubicle you know). The results were submitted as evidence and the verdict had to be passed, here and now.

My conclusion: I'm pretty sure I must have blacked out. There is no way I could have slipped. The angles and the science were against that theory. The only way I could have banged the right side of my head would have been to fall to my right, making it impossible to have been walking towards the door. I could've only been facing the wall standing at the toilet or the back wall. To have hit my head where I hit it, I would've collapsed and fallen straight down and hit my head on the edge of the sink or toilet. That was it! Case closed!

After trying not to outstay my welcome in the toilet cubicle, I made my way back into the restaurant and re-joined Jules who was waiting anxiously to make sure I was ok.

We had a few tears and then decided to share with the family on our WhatsApp group what had happened. As I was about to post something, an email notification popped through to give us the news that we were finalists at the SME Awards. Talk about emotions. Relief, answers, excitement and pride all in one go.

You'll be pleased to know that my toilet CSI reconstructions pretty much stopped after visiting Fuerteventura almost six years after the accident, but there was still one final piece of the jigsaw to be locked into place before moving on. By complete accident, I found it during another trip, this time to Majorca.

If ever I spoke about the incident, '*I suffered a head injury*' would normally be followed by the question, '*what happened?*'

Of course, people are inquisitive and curious. I used to get asked if I got attacked, was I drunk or did I black-out? These were all great questions, but I'd normally have to answer that I didn't know. Some people would accept that answer, others would show a little disappointment that the story was incomplete, and a few would start their own construction of events. The latter was always, well maybe this or maybe that. To be fair, that never hugely bothered me. In years of personal development, I've learned to accept that it doesn't matter what people think. As long as it's not going to cause any long-term issues then that's cool. They would soon move onto something else of focus very soon anyway. This wouldn't stop me wondering what happened though. What the hell happened? Why did I fall and hit my head?

So, onto our next trip to Majorca. We sat eating our evening meal at a lovely hotel in Santa Ponsa. It was the last evening of a short break. We'd run the Palma 10K and half marathon the day before and enjoyed a little autumn sunshine. It was a lovely relaxing break (Ok, some of you may not describe running around a capital city as relaxing but it was part of our active and relaxing lifestyle). One of my favourite types of food is buffet food, so I headed back to the spread for a second potion of main course (running makes you extra hungry of course). Paella... nice.

Halfway through my plateful of food, I realised that the paella contained squid. Now without boring you with lots of details, Jules and I are vegetarian and stopped eating fish years before. Also, we're not too precious on sweating the small stuff and causing a scene, so my immediate solution was to finish the food.

Just to throw another small (and key) fact in here, a number of years ago I found out I suffered a digestion problem and had cameras put into parts of my body that you don't want to think about (stay with me on this, it will make sense in a moment). The hospital found that I have a small defect in my gullet, and this can affect me swallowing food causing acid reflux. It's actually quite common and not dangerous but some foods can irritate this condition. Guess what, one of them is squid.

After eating the paella and picking out bits of squid, my throat closed up and I was finding it hard to swallow at this point. Oh no, it's a little embarrassing. I wanted some water. I went to the bar but there was nobody around. We needed some water for the evening so I decided to pop over to the supermarket opposite the hotel and hopefully my blocked throat would clear. Jules stayed at the table and finished eating.

I wandered over the road and, as I entered the store, my head was spinning and my throat hiccupping. I paid for the large bottle of water and left the shop. Finding the closest wall, I sat there and felt as if I was going to pass out. It was horrible. Have you ever felt faint? That moment when the blood rushes away from your head and you go all wobbly. I drank some water, but it wouldn't get past my throat. Discreetly I spat it into the flower bed behind me and tried to drink more. The result was the same and the flowers were watered again. A couple of minutes later, thankfully, the blockage cleared, and my spinning world started to clear.

"Where have you been?" Jules was worried of course. I'd been gone far too long just to get a bottle of water from a shop that was less than 100 yards away. Sometimes I'd be off chatting to someone or something but I didn't know anyone here, so the concern was natural.

Do you ever watch a TV programme and think, where is all this going? Well here's the aha moment. What did I eat before I went to the toilet in Fuerteventura six years before? Yep, squid!

That's it! Watson, we have solved the mystery, Holmes said triumphantly. My reconstruction was now complete. Could we really close the case now? Here's detective Mark's conclusion:

We sat in a small tapas bar and ate our starter. Part way through the squid dish, my throat closed up due to the allergy. Without wanting to make an issue of it, I went to the toilet. Standing in the cubicle, the blood rushed from my head and I blacked out, causing me to fall to my right. My head hit the sink causing severe trauma to my skull on the right side.

There you go. The statement could now be released to the press in the six-year long investigation. OK, there may still be case for appeal or conspiracy but, in my mind, I'm now 99% satisfied that this is what happened. Sorted. Please note: I still have no recollection of what I just said but feel it's as close to the truth as I'll ever get.

Jules also agreed with my theory and we decided that was good enough to move on from this question that had bugged us both for years. I can't tell you how much of a relief it is to get closure on a question that's been playing on your mind for so long. With that step out of the way, it would just be the case of removing some of the anxiety and rollercoaster of high then low then high then boom. Easy? I wish!

Chapter 25: Jules

Our flight down to southern India was a bit of a nightmare. We were delayed leaving Heathrow, therefore missed our connection in Kuwait to Cochin in India. We had to spend 24 hours cooped up in a hotel at the airport waiting for the next available flight, but we made it. We stayed in Fort Cochin then travelled down to Vakarla on the wonderful Indian train system. It was just as you'd imagine it to be, although the air-con packed up and we kinda melted. What an experience though, and the scenery was fabulous. We headed back up to Cochin and caught a flight to Sri Lanka. Whilst here we went on boat trips watching whales and dolphins, and went on a safari which was just incredible being so close to these animals in their natural habitat. We just loved every minute of it except that Mark couldn't keep his anxiety under control the whole time.

It was the first time in all of our travels that it really got to Mark. Other times in new places he would have what I call little wobbles, but this holiday was different. Right from the start in Heathrow airport I could see he was a bag of nerves. It wasn't that he was a nervous flyer, we'd flown so many times, but this was different. It was like he was scared of everything. I know that often when we're away and people talk to us in either broken English or their language, Mark struggles to understand what they're saying but I always manage to work out what's going on. However this time it was really getting to him, he was edgy all the time and was visibly shaking.

When we go on our longer travels, we generally book any flights beforehand, with an idea of whereabouts we want to visit. We'd have the first few days' accommodation sorted, which is what we'd done on this trip. The couple at our first homestay were really great to us. They helped us book our train journey to Vakarla and organised us an Uber to get us to the station on the day we were ready to go. Mark had begun to relax a little here and I wondered if the train would faze him, but he wasn't too bad once we got on board. Whenever we were out and about visiting an area, walking or buying lunch or coffee, he really went into himself and I could see him shaking. I didn't a make a big thing of it, as I knew it would make him worse and I so wanted him to enjoy this glorious place. I could sense the immense struggle he was having within himself, so I kept holding his hand, hugging him and telling him that I loved him.

It was time to fly to Sri Lanka! I couldn't wait, it was only a 50-minute flight on one of the biggest aeroplanes ever. I'd helped Mark through the crazy check-in and security procedures and just kept hold of his hand to make sure he knew where to go and what to do, while giving him reassurance that everything was ok.

Once we were up in the air and Mark had calmed somewhat, we chatted about our next adventures and he looked at me and said,

"I just wish I could I get rid of this anxiety!"

"Me too" I replied.

His hands were still trembling and he couldn't think of any reason as to why he was feeling so bad and nervous.

We stayed one night in the capital, Colombo, and then headed to a place called Bentota for a few days. Our hotel was just incredible, it was like going back hundreds of years. We ate breakfast and dinner on the lawns that overlooked the river coming in from the sea, idyllic.

On the second day there, we went for a walk and found a shop that sold trips, so we went to investigate what was available. One of the things was to go to a turtle sanctuary and the guy's dad could take us straightaway in his tuk-tuk. Yes, I'm in! How wonderful, but oh my goodness, Mark's face! He looked horrified, almost like, what now, this minute, I need to think about this, I can't cope with this and I'm not ready to go. I sat him down and gently said,

"We have nothing planned, it's something we said we'd like to do and why not today? If we do this today then that will give us time to do the other things and we can plan them later. Please let's just go, I know you'll have a great time."

Thankfully he agreed but he did need a lot of persuading. All that lovely spontaneity he used to have was gone and replaced with fear instead. I felt incredibly sad for him and held his hand even tighter. However, we did have just the most incredible time with those beautiful turtles, tickling their tummies and holding them. We even saw some hatch!

We were then heading further south to a place called Marissa. Again, a heavenly little place with the friendliest homestay ever, where they looked after us so well. The husband drove us to a safari park. The lady delighted in serving us up different foods for breakfast, as she could see we were loving it. She gave me books to read; nothing was too much trouble and they were such humble, caring people. The area was gorgeous and had everything you wanted: a stunning beach and wonderful scenery, some lovely shops and restaurants, surely nothing could spoil it?

I delighted in enjoying the local culture and watching them live such a simple life and Mark tried his best too, but he was still afraid of almost everything. Walking down the road was difficult, as footpaths were sparse. It seemed like he was struggling to judge distances of how far away a car or bike was from us and panicking at the slightest thing. One evening we went out for something to eat and to be fair we probably didn't pick the best place, but it was full of people enjoying themselves so we thought it must be good.

We ordered beers and food then Mark became quite edgy,

"Let's go", I said "I can see you're not too happy about this choice so let's just go."

He wouldn't and said it was ok to stay. Our food took a little while to come and Mark was getting more agitated. Afterwards he went to find the loo, actually he was gone a little while and I did start to worry a little (wonder why!) but he appeared back, phew!

However, he didn't look brilliant, he had that lost look on his face and his eyes seemed very blank.

"Come on, let's get back," I insisted.

It was really hard work getting him there, he jumped at every tiny little noise. Once we got on the main road, he believed every car, lorry or bus was going to hit him. I had to hold him tight to my side on the inside of the road and convince him they were miles away so I could get him back to our place. Once there he lay down on the bed and I fell asleep only to be woken up a short while later by the sound of him being violently sick in the toilet. Bloody anxiety had him tied up again. It took a lot of gentle persuading but eventually he got back into bed and we managed to get some rest. In the morning he couldn't remember what had happened. He recalled going for food and feeling uneasy about the place and the rest was a complete blur.

I came to realise that the issues we were having were because everything was new and unfamiliar, and this unsettled him even more so on this trip. This behaviour had already manifested itself long ago. If we wanted to change anything or do something new, maybe in our school sessions for example, I'd have to work really hard for Mark to accept the change. He'd often agree the idea was great, but putting it into practice wasn't so easy. I would literally have to go over and over it at least 10-15 times before eventually it would settle in his memory and we could proceed. We were taking steps forward, yes, they were small steps, but they were in the right direction.

Chapter 26: Mark

This was wiping me out now. Functioning day to day was becoming more difficult. Ok, I was able to do all the physical things but mentally, well, it just got harder. The highs were still there; we went off to travel around India and Sri Lanka for Christmas along with other exciting things. Trouble was, the lows were just too frequent. Where had my confidence gone? Why were we not going to social events anymore? How come I'm forgetting things so frequently? Why am I snapping at Jules so often? My energy was so low. I wanted to sleep so often. Then I'd go to bed at night, have hideous nightmares and then lie awake. All I wanted to do was run off and go travelling. That's the time when I felt most relaxed.

That whole theory of travelling and feeling relaxed was blown out of the water as we landed in India to start a month-long adventure. We started the trip in Ealing the night before flying out from Heathrow. I was a mess in my mind. Everything felt scary. I was worrying about missing the flight, getting refused entry on our visa or losing my passport. For someone who travels so regularly, this wasn't like me.

Two days later, we were in Fort Kochin, after an unexpected overnight delay in Kuwait, and the adventure began.

India was magical. The sights, the people, the food... it was an incredible experience. Trouble was, I couldn't relax. We'd be walking along a beautiful beach in Varkala and suddenly I'd be struggling to breathe. Why? The place was amazing! I was with Jules, the person I most wanted to share this moment with. It didn't make sense.

Two weeks later we made the short flight to Sri Lanka and we were both so excited. This place had been on our bucket list for ages and our dream was about to become a reality.

On the plane, I squeezed Jules's hand and said, "Babe, I'm so excited but I need to shake this anxiety. I don't know what's wrong with me!"

We chatted away on the flight and I felt calm when we landed. I knew how much of a pain I felt and how upsetting this all was for Jules, but I couldn't allow this to get in the way of our adventure. Trouble is, the mind state was overtaking everything now and I didn't understand why.

After a bit of a panic at the airport, I felt fine as we'd cleared customs and headed off on the next part of our adventure. Sri Lanka for the most part was different. I felt a lot calmer and embraced the sheer beauty of this place. The people are the humblest people we'd ever met, and they touched our hearts with their genuine kindness and smiles. Other than a couple of meltdowns, I loved this part of our trip and felt at home.

It felt a little easier to open up to Jules as we visited the west followed by the south of this beautiful island. No longer could I hold all this mentally sapping anxiety inside me anymore. I couldn't continue the unpredictable highs and lows and the upset it was causing us both. This cycle was getting all too familiar. Another year had passed, and things weren't improving. Now I couldn't do anything without a side effect. What started with disrupted concentration and a little tiredness was now fully blown out of proportion. Truth is, the small changes weren't obvious in the early days as I held back from telling anyone how I felt to protect them from worrying about me. Couple that with not actually admitting there's an issue and thinking this would pass; I'd just been sweeping stuff underneath the rug. Trouble is, there was so much crap underneath the rug now, it was practically touching the ceiling. What was the answer?

Again, we thought that there was hope that help could be on the way. Some three months earlier, I'd made another trip to the doctors. It was time for another shot but this time without the bravado of the fit, active, motivational speaker, business owner, runner etc. This time, I needed to be the poor, helpless, lost boy who was suffering.

Now our doctor's surgery is great. They listen and act. This visit was no different. The doctor referred me to the neurologist at Northampton General Hospital again and I decided that I was going to let loose on all of the issues. There'd be no holding back and pretending everything was OK. It was almost six years to the day since the incident and, without being an expert, I don't think this brain was going to heal itself now. As always, the consultant was really welcoming, caring and open. However, this was also a pretty scary visit. In the room were two student nurses who were probably just as nervous as I was. I found it hard to talk about everything, but I managed to get my point across.

The result was a referral for an MRI scan to take a look at my brain. The results showed there was still scarring to my right temporal lobe consistent with the previous scans. But that was it again, nothing. I received a letter with my results and then nothing. It just seemed that it is the way it is. The consultant actually used the phrase that my injury was '*spectacular*' and said that, '*people don't survive this, never mind survive it and are able to live their lives*!' Great, I feel lucky, but it doesn't help when you're still dealing with this crap every single day.

I just kept thinking, where do I go from here? I've been to doctors, been to hospital and always ended back at square one. It was like an impossible game of snakes and ladders. I just knew that I couldn't go through it all again and let this consume me anymore.

Chapter 27: Jules

We got back to the UK just in time to see the New Year in, but I'll be honest, I wasn't as excited about a brand-new year as I should have been. My niece messaged to say they were having a party and we were invited. Yes I thought, how wonderful! It's been absolutely years since I'd spent a NYE with my brother, and my sister could make it for a few hours too. Oh, but Mark didn't want to go. I'd arranged that we could sleep there so we could both relax but he was dead against it,

"What if I get tired, what if it's too noisy?" he kept saying.

"What if you enjoy it, what if we have some fun?" I asked.

In the end the compromise was that he would drive us there so we could leave if he felt tired. Within half an hour I looked at him and saw that all too familiar face that showed he wasn't happy, his face was pale, and I'd lost him, gutted! I was a little annoyed; I thought that because he said he '*might*' feel like this, he almost talked himself into feeling wiped out as soon as we arrived. So, we left after a short while and came home to bed.

I wanted desperately to get some help with Mark, we just couldn't keep going on as we were, and I wanted him to go back to the doctors or his neurologist again. The thought of another year of bouncing from deep despair to joy to deep despair filled me with a sense of hopelessness. I didn't know what that help looked like, but I was sure there had to be some kind of therapy and medication that could help him get back on an even keel. The mention of medication never went down too well with him. He was fearful of side effects that he'd heard about, but I just thought if they helped him feel better about himself and if we could just find someone to help him with some coping mechanisms then we might be ok.

It was extremely sad to see the man I had met all those years ago almost withering away before my eyes. His OCD was worse than ever, the cycle of fatigue and resting, rather than making him feel better, only seemed to make him feel guiltier and worse than before. He'd seen his neurologist back in September 2018, had an MRI scan and something else for the nerve issues he had developed in his fingers. Once more it just confirmed he has scarring on his brain consistent with the injury he'd sustained in 2012.

January 2019 and we'd had quite a few school workshops with two of them to be presented in the prestigious Barclaycard offices here in Northampton. We both particularly loved delivering these, not just because of the professional surroundings, but the buzz we got from the teenagers along with awesome feedback from them and the teachers present.

It was coming up for my birthday in early February and I mildly joked with Mark as it got closer, not to make me cry and upset me like he had the previous year! As a child you're told to blow out the candles on your cake and make a wish. I didn't care if I had a birthday cake or any candles for that matter, but if I had one wish it would be to get my husband back.

So there I was on the sofa, three days before my birthday with a throw over my head, inconsolably crying, asking Mark to just go away and leave me alone. I was broken, felt beyond any repair and had no idea what the hell just happened?

I laid there after he'd left and contemplated our future. I did almost decide that yes, I was going to leave him. I didn't feel I had anything left to give him; our whole lives just evolved around making his life better, day after day, week after week. We'd cancelled so many social events as he couldn't cope with going. I held him up when he was feeling so down, I'd sat with him whilst he was being sick, I'd listened to him cry himself to sleep, I did as much work as I could possibly do with our business to take some strain off him, I did all the house work, shopping and cooking and I loved him. What else could I do?

Roxanne and the three grandsons were coming down two days later but instead I started to plan to go up there, even if it was just to get away from Mark for a few days. However I knew that wasn't the right thing to do, as that would only increase his sense of failure and despair and I just couldn't do that to him.

I got up in the morning and slipped out of the house up to Daniel's house and poured my heart out to him over copious amounts of coffee. I felt much better and able to face everything again so came home. Mark was quiet and withdrawn and looked pale. We had a little hug and asked if each other was ok and I told him where I'd been. It wasn't until a little later I plucked up the courage to ask him if he still felt the same about us breaking up.

He looked shocked and asked me what I meant. I told him that's what he wanted last night. He had absolutely no recollection of saying it, he knew something awful had happened but couldn't piece it together or recall the events.

This upset me greatly and, as always, frustrated me. Many times I've fought back the feeling of '*Oh yeah that old chestnut, if I say I can't remember then everything will be alright*' but it happens so often I know he genuinely can't remember. It also seems the more emotional it is then the less likely he is to remember it. He said that he's so sorry for what occurred and said most definitely it's not what he wants to do; he said he couldn't live without me. I then begged the question,

"So what are we going to do about it? I seriously I think we need to go to the doctors and talk medication!"

He actually agreed. He also had a long and deep conversation with Roxanne again while she was down which helped him. She too felt that he needed get some therapeutic help and medication but knew that this was a big sticking point with him, and it was a route he didn't want to take.

I think he realised though that he definitely needed help and did try calling the doctors a couple of times but could never get an answer.

He eventually got an appointment to see his neurologist for the 20th February. I believed for the first time he actually confessed to how bad he was mentally, and lo and behold, he was offered the opportunity to see a clinical psychologist at the Brain Injury Service at a hospital about ten miles from where we live. We were actually stunned that we didn't know that this place even existed or that we hadn't been told about it at any of the previous appointments we'd had. But I strongly believed that at the last couple of appointments he'd been to on his own, he hadn't fully told them of how bad our situation was, otherwise I'm sure they would've referred us earlier. However, it is what it is and at least things were moving in the right direction.

We got our appointment to see the Psychologist on 29th March. I was invited along too which I was so grateful for and we spent almost two hours with her telling our story. She was amazed at what we'd been through and where we were, so put a care plan into place immediately for him. She also highly recommended we go and see our local doctor and get some medication but to this date he still hasn't wanted to do this.

I'm ok with this now because since we had that appointment he's begun to change. Mark's been able to start talking more freely about his mental health and to more than just me. He's spoken to some friends and family and is beginning to lose that feeling of embarrassment about what's happened. It's also shocked him that people have said how he's such a changed person and so quiet compared to what he used to be. He's almost in disbelief and can't see how different he's become. It's also good that he's hearing this from other people and not just me. The talking is starting to work wonders and he's becoming more relaxed and open about how he's been feeling and the anguish he's gone through. I've been able to tell him truthfully how he's made me feel. How at times I didn't believe him and thought he was making it up to suit him. How I thought I was going mad and imagining it all and that it was my fault.

I could now tell him what my sons have said. In particular, one of their friends who'd come to visit recently and hadn't seen Mark in a couple of years. Straight after leaving us, he'd turned to Russell in their car and said,

"OK, what going on with Mark? That isn't the man I know and met years ago."

I know it's really hard for him to hear these stories, but we both know it's helping him come to terms with where he is. We can now spend hours talking and reliving the difficult moments. It's great for me not having the constant feeling of, '*Well I can't say that because he'll just go into a downward spiral again and I'll lose him for a few days.*'

The first thing the Brain Injury Service did was to invite him onto a Fatigue Management group, and he's gone along to quite a lot of the meetings. This has helped him immensely in understanding what he's going through and how to cope with it mentally and physically.

I haven't got a happy-ever-after ending to our story for you, as Mark still struggles daily with the anxiety but he's managing to deal with it a whole lot better than before. He still needs to rest loads but we both recognise the signs and adjust our days accordingly. We're currently awaiting the dates for us to have sessions with a psychologist and for the first time in a few years, we feel hopeful for the future. We know the side effects from his injury, the fatigue, the memory loss, the anxiety and changes in his mood will never go away. But we're slowly coming to terms with and working on living with these. We hope with the help of his own psychologist, we can get more coping mechanisms in place.

I'm also acutely aware that as I'm writing this we are in the school holidays and once it starts back and we begin to have the busy schedules, things could very easily and quickly take a turn backwards, but for the moment we're happy and smiling again. I'm even back doing my silly dances and singing in the kitchen!

I had no idea what anxiety or depression looked like, I'd never experienced it and nor had Mark. We also had no idea that this was in fact very common and quite normal as a result of his injury. We thought we could cope with it and were often told in the early years after his injury that these symptoms would mostly disappear.

Because of dealing with the sudden passing of my dear mum, then my illness and subsequent awful effects of the chemotherapy, I hadn't taken enough time to notice just how bad and how far Mark had slipped into this deep hole. By the time I had realised it was almost too late, he was in such a dark place and I had no skills or knowledge of how to help him.

Mark made the mistake of bottling his feelings up and not letting on how much the anxiety was taking hold through this time and it continued long after I'd realised where we were.

Looking back, I should've pushed harder and gone to the last couple of visits with Mark to his neurologist and explained our situation. However, I didn't, and Mark didn't fully tell them the whole picture until after I broke down and he thought he'd lost me. Maybe I should have gone to my GP and explained the situation and asked for help. There were many times when I should have had more patience with Mark and also many times when he should have opened up and explained how he was feeling and what was going on in his head.

One thing I know is that there is no shame in depression or anxiety, but the need to talk is paramount in getting the help and support needed. It is indeed OK not be OK. Mental health is destroying families, marriages, and friendships because there is still the taboo about admitting you're not OK. Word is slowly getting out there, but we all need to be mindful of our nearest and dearest and if you're noticing some changes, help them to talk before it gets to the point where we were and it almost destroyed a wonderful happy marriage.

I came up with idea of putting this in writing as I laid in bed one night and decided '*I need to get this story out there.*' There must be hundreds of people going through something similar and I wanted to share this and our mistakes so that they don't have to go through the depths of despair that we have.

Putting this book together has helped us to piece our journey together and Mark has found it profoundly useful. I won't lie, it's been hard! We've shed many tears, but it's made us face the truth and realise how much your mental health can have such serious consequences on your relationships. It's also brought us back together to a place that I didn't think we could get to. It just shows you what the power of talking, writing and releasing your emotions, can really do.

We know we're not at the end of this yet and I fear there still may be some tears in the future. We've made a commitment to each other to be honest, talk about how we're feeling and how we're going to look after ourselves. This is so we can indeed grow old together, dance in the kitchen, hug those adorable grandkids, swim in the world's oceans, climb those mountains and love life.

If you're reading this and you are in a similar place, please don't leave it. It's OK to ask for help as it won't go away on its own. There are so many avenues now for getting the right help and I just wish we did it years ago. If sharing our story can help just one person to recognise the signs and symptoms of anxiety and/or depression and can seek help before it really takes hold, then we know writing this has been worth it.

A message for Mark:
To my wonderful HubbaHubba, words cannot describe the depth of love I have for you and always will. From the moment we got together you have filled my life full of love and laughter. You understand me like no other and have given me the belief, courage and confidence in myself to do things I would never have dreamed I could achieve, and I thank you from the bottom of my heart. You are my husband, my best friend, my true soul mate and my lover.

I thank the lucky stars each and every day that you chose me to be your wife and to whatever force was with us that fateful day you had the accident and survived, as without you I am nothing.

I truly believe that we're now even stronger and closer on our journey through life together than ever before and I am so proud of you to be able to share our story with me.

A message to anyone who loves someone who has suffered a brain injury:

Have patience and understanding; it's very difficult and hard to comprehend the situation you're in. Seek as much help and support that you can to help you to help your loved one. They do not wish to cause you any pain and often are completely unaware of their behaviour and, under *'normal'* circumstances, wouldn't behave in the way they are now. Above all else talk to each other as much as you can and listen to each other. That way, you can get a better understanding of what is happening and how to support each other.

Chapter 28: Mark

So, let me take you back to the beginning of this book when I was wondering what the hell just happened? Why was I thinking that Jules would be better off without me upsetting her all the time, making her angry and irritated? That endless cycle I've mentioned a lot, goes round and round and round! High, low... lower... anxious... no self-esteem, then Jules would snap at me for what I thought was no reason. There would be no hug, no kiss... I'd then just think, '*Oh great, what have I done now*?'

When Jules told me that I'd suggested that we part, I was stunned! What? Did I really say that? Why? This is absolutely the last thing I would ever want. Wow, I've just actually felt anxious writing that. This is when my brain and I fall out because that is not the person I am. In all of the low points of this journey, this is absolutely the worst for me. It's worse than the days after the accident. Worse than the night in John Radcliffe Hospital. And I tell you, those were bad! I can accept most things that have happened and move on from them, but this is the hardest of all. Breaking up our marriage is unthinkable.

I'd felt so lost for so long and I didn't know what to do for the best. All I knew was that I couldn't do this anymore. I couldn't do this to Jules anymore. I couldn't do this to my friends anymore. We'd recently been to a party and I had to sit in the corner again and then slip out when everyone started having a bit of fun. Yep, the music gets a little louder, a bit of dancing begins, and we make an excuse that we need to leave. Where had the happy and carefree Mark gone?

Another example was, a friend said he'd pick me up one Saturday morning at a certain time but I hadn't got the confidence to ask him why he was picking me up. It turned out that we were off to a running event (I knew that bit) but didn't remember where. My brain had shut off again and I'd forgotten important details.

I'd had enough of these moments when I was unable to remember parts a conversation or I'd be in a meeting and have to battle to concentrate.

Enough was enough! It was time to speak out, time to stop holding back and time to deal with it. Let's stop being a bloke for a while and stop hiding and pretending. To be honest, it was sooo bloody obvious, I couldn't even fool the most naive person now. It was clear that something was wrong.

I rang the hospital.

"Yep, this is just a call to follow up on my scan."

"Certainly, let's get you booked in. Can you do 19th February?"

Just like that! No questions. I had an appointment with the neurologist consultant again. Simple. Trouble is, where was this going to go? Would I get the same response as before? Who knows?

The day arrived and I expected Jules to come to the hospital with me, but she told me to go on my own. I felt a little dejected because I just needed a safety net. I felt alone and anxious.

After the blood pressure readings were given, I knew it wasn't the time to celebrate my fitness. I returned to my seat in the waiting room. No sooner had my backside made contact with the chair, my name was called. I wandered into the consultant's office to be greeted with his usual friendly smile and a handshake.

"So, you've come to talk about the results of your MRI scan? Let's take a look at how we can help you."

There was no reading through any notes or pause for thought, he came straight out with it and suggested a referral to a brain psychologist at the Community Brain Injury clinic. I was stunned! Stunned with relief! This was good news! Psychologist sounded like someone who could help and the words community, brain injury and clinic sounded like the place to get support. I was expecting to have to travel to somewhere like John Radcliffe Hospital in Oxford or something, but was even more surprised when he told me it was at Isebrook Hospital in Wellingborough. This is less than 10 miles from our home!

We chatted some more, and I felt like I'd reached a breakthrough but my excitement was knocked back down a little with a warning. There was no guarantee that they would agree to see me because... yep, fit, active, mobile, amazing survivor... you know the story. However, he told me that he'd do everything he could to get me an appointment and I trusted that he would.

Six weeks later, Jules and I sat with a Clinical Psychologist in the Community Brain Injury Clinic at Isebrook Hospital. The one-hour appointment ended up being close to two hours. We told our story from both sides; the list came out and almost everything was covered. You know when you blow up a balloon and then let it go without tying the end? It flies around the room before falling deflated in the corner. That was me that day. The pressure released, I spun around with excitement and then flopped out on the bed and slept for about two hours when we got home.

How to describe the feelings now? Still scared, not sure what to expect. Relieved, help is finally on its way. A fraud, yeah... fit and active and all that... Excited, perhaps I'm approaching the corner that needs to be turned. Worried, what if it's a big let-down and I end up back at square one again?

Five weeks after my appointment with the Psychologist, my care plan letter arrived. I could attend various support groups including Understanding Brain Injury and Fatigue Management. I was also on the waiting list to see the Psychologist.

This all felt right! For the first time I actually felt as though I could move on beyond this anxiety that had been building over six and a half years. My whole emotion changed and suddenly I could start talking to Jules about how I felt. Crazy that, I share absolutely everything with her and we have the most honest and loving relationship anyone could wish for. Now these deep-rooted issues could start to be pulled apart.

When we moved into the house we live in, our neighbours decided to take down an ivy bush that had grown up the side of their house and had pretty much consumed a whole fence panel. I went to help them one day and the whole root stretched from one side of their garden to the far corner, it was about 15 metres long. We hacked and chopped bits off of it for days until it was finally removed. The ivy has barely grown since. This could be the same as my anxiety, stress and the whole feeling of hopelessness. Bit by bit, the deep roots could be removed.

One day it happened. Another pressure valve was released. The pressure valve of emotion! We were away and had been chatting about a sad issue in our family. Later that evening, after dinner, we were out. Suddenly I started feeling an overwhelming fog surrounding me and the confusion began to kick in. This was a familiar yet scary feeling. Space becomes distorted, what's on the other side of the room seems to be right in front of me. Noise distorts and I'm aware that my voice is slurred and words aren't stringing together. Nope, I wasn't drunk before you ask, it's just a common side effect of brain injury!

The next thing I remember, I'm sitting on the sofa in our apartment and Jules has her arms around me as I was crying, completely inconsolable. This moment seemed to last for hours but it felt safe. Jules's hug was tight, comforting and secure. We went to bed and I must have immediately fell asleep, not waking until the next morning.

As I opened my eyes, the sun was shining. I felt calm and relaxed. The anxiety was nowhere to be seen. Jules smiled her usual smile at me and we just hugged again. This pressure valve of emotion was now open and it had to stay that way. This was the first time I felt I'd been able to properly let everything go. There was absolutely no way

I could allow that valve to shut. I felt like I'd got my wife back and perhaps I could be that person I once was for her too.

Weeks later, I attended my Fatigue Management session at Isebrook Hospital. Being honest, I was anxious on the morning. Arriving and taking my seat, everyone introduced themselves. There was a guy who'd been assaulted 20 years ago, a retired gentleman recovering from a stroke (with his wife), a man who fell off the back of a lorry (not stolen, he actually tumbled) and a young lady who survived meningitis (and her mum).

The awkward moment came when I introduced myself as an author and motivational speaker who runs two businesses. These guys needed physical care and I didn't. The lovely man who'd had the stroke was walking with a stick and I was talking about doing a parkrun at the weekend. After about 15 minutes, I came clean and told the group that I felt a bit of a fraud here and guilty that I was able to do so much. That awkwardness was then removed forever.

Janette, the mum of Kirsty, who survived meningitis, turned to me and said,

"You're here for a reason and that is because you're suffering as much as all of these people in the room. You need this as much as they do so don't feel guilty."

I could've cried! For the first time it felt it was OK to be getting support. I think there's so much stigma with counselling that people shy away from it, especially in Britain where the phrase '*Keep Calm and Carry On*' has been resurrected in recent years. American TV or film glamorise that it's cool to have a shrink (as they call it) but I'm sure it's not. I find that men are especially private when it comes to talking about mental health. In our business, we encourage people to be open and honest with themselves but it's not that easy to do it yourself.

The help and support at Isebrook has been amazing so far. The Fatigue Management group is the only place where it's acceptable to yawn while the facilitator is talking! Yep, that joke got a few smiles. I feel at home there because I've got the added bonus of being able to offer my knowledge and studies from the world of self-help and personal development to others, but also realise I'm there as a patient.

It's wonderful, I've already been asked to be involved and speak at some of their events but I will take this part one step at a time. Instead of flying around at 100mph, I now drop my speed to 50mph or even park up, put on the handbrake and assess it from time to time. It's amazing that at times it feels fine and acceptable to say no. To be able to decline an offer without the feeling of letting someone down. Only a week before writing this part, I was honoured to be asked to be part of a local public speaking group and mentor others on one of the scariest acts in the world (yes, public speaking is feared more than death by some). I parked up, popped on the handbrake and said, thank you for the opportunity but not at the moment.

I've also learnt more about the side effects of brain injuries and the best analogy is like the app on a mobile phone. Imagine that you have a mobile phone with a low battery and you're running lots of apps at once. The battery will drain quicker and the phone will slow down. The brain is exactly the same. When my brain tries to send a signal from A to B, it may not be able to take the most direct route and will fly around causing overload. This is why I struggle to process lots of information at one time. What a brilliant way of understanding what's happening. If I'm feeling tired or overloaded now, I just say I'm buffering. It's also easier for Jules to tell me I'm buffering when she notices before I do. It feels a lot softer and a more fun way of explaining that I need a rest.

Everyone loves a story with a happy ending, but I can't give you that. I'm still on our journey. Our journey never stops but it's better to have one that you can enjoy. However, I can give you a wonderful ending to where we are at the present time.

I feel that we're getting our life back. Only a few weeks ago we sat in the conservatory and played random music on a playlist. Jules was dancing around the room as I was busy selecting the next song. Her moves were great and her smile was huge as she danced, pushing her hair up. We laughed and laughed and before I knew it tears of joy were rolling down my face! It was a beautiful moment that will stay in my heart forever. This is how we used to be, and these moments are becoming more and more regular.

Our life is going back to the days before all of these challenges zapped us. Before brain injury, grief of losing my mother-in-law and the challenges of breast cancer. We will never recover fully of course. Some people say time is a healer for grief but that hurt will never go away.

I know Jules was hit by her illness and still bears the scars. She made an amazing recovery both physically and mentally, but she's also sometimes tired and struggles to focus. She suffers pain following her many operations and, of course, the worry that this illness returning causes. I know that she wouldn't be able to go back to running multiple training centres like she used to. Being honest, I'm glad of that. People get stuck in the '*have to*' lifestyle instead of the '*want to*' and we've made changes to make sure that Jules doesn't have that stress in her life.

And of course, brain injury has changed me forever. I accept that I won't be able to give everybody my full attention and focus but I have no problem explaining that to them now. Processing instructions and information sometimes isn't going to happen as my short-term memory doesn't function properly. In fact, give me too much information and my brain will shut down completely. And of course, there's fatigue. Many years ago, my mum had a mirror with an old fashioned Coca Cola advert on it. In big letters it had the words "Relieves Fatigue" across it. I used to read it out and pronounce it 'rell-eves fatty-gew'. I'm not sure that the claims of this drink are technically correct, but little did I know that some 40-odd years later, my life would be dominated by the word fatigue (or fatty-gew'). The wonderful people at Isebrook gave me a great tip to rest on good days as well as tired days, so that's what I do now.

I will feel emotional, confused and anxiety will still kick in at times, but it's happening less and less now. The right side of my head will hurt pretty much every day. Sometimes it will feel as if I've been struck with a large object and other times it will just be a dull ache. Loud noises and flashing lights, busy rooms and lots of movement can disturb my sense of spatial awareness but that's the way it is. Life has to be adapted to deal with these things.

In a short space of time, I've made some huge steps. Finally getting support is obviously a major help but having the ability to be honest and open is the biggest one of all. I can talk openly to Jules and tell her that I need to go home, rest or even sit in a certain place in public to avoid lots of noise. What's more, I can take her advice when I'm flagging. Yes guys, listen to your nearest and dearest, they know best!

Joking aside though, Jules spends a lot of time with me, we work together and live together. Now I can understand when she tells me to rest, get off the computer, go to bed early or whatever is going to work. If we're having a business meeting, I can deflect the conversation to Jules and even be honest with the person we're meeting with in order to avoid information overload.

It's a huge relief to talk to family and friends now without the fear of, '*Oh here comes the brain injury card now.*' On that note, I actually do have a brain injury card from Headway. The card lists some side effects including difficulties with concentration, following instructions, processing information and fatigue. It's designed to be able to present to anyone in public to explain the situation should any difficulties arise. As yet, it stays tucked safely in my wallet just in case. It's actually acted as a reminder to me to sometimes slow down or take a step back.

Recently I read an article about Olympian and celebrity, James Cracknell, who suffered a head injury whilst cycling. He talks about his marriage ending because he became a different person, suffering with a change in personality. People may throw judgement out there and say something like, '*It's ok for him, he's got loads of money.*'

The bottom line is, we all have a brain and it doesn't matter who we are, it's one of the most complicated organs in our body.

Reading this made me feel lucky to have come out the other side with such a wonderful wife. I may have pushed her to the edge at times and I feel incredibly guilty for that. I always go back to the point; this isn't either of our faults. We have to deal with it.

Being in the world of personal development and positivity, there are two choices in life. You complain and be the victim or you take the positive outlook. There's enough rubbish in the world and the media does a very good job of filling us with doom, gloom, negativity and hate. Jules and I ignore that, we never watch the news, read the papers or watch reality TV shows. That breeds the victim culture. Instead, we read positive books, listen to and watch motivational stories from people who have achieved amazing things. We hang around smiley, happy people and spend time doing things that we like to do.

I could play the victim card and so could Jules. We could continue along the lines of '*why me*?' Don't get me wrong, I've felt sorry for myself many times throughout the past few years but that doesn't work. I could complain that it's taken me over six years to get some help and support and start blaming the hospital or Headway for turning me away but why would I do that? The NHS employ wonderful people who care and Headway are an amazing charity. They're both overstretched by the system and have to make a snapshot decision under pressure.

My advice to anyone in this situation is not to walk away if you really need support. Keep calm and keep asking. There is no point flying through the door, arms waving and shouting. Simply explain how you feel and be strong and persistent.

My biggest downfalls were my self-doubt and bottling up how I felt. Share, share, share... If I didn't understand what was going on in my head, how could I expect my wife, family and friends to understand?

Don't be a secret agent. James Bond may be a cool character but when it comes to mental health, you can't hide behind being a 007 character.

So, I'm still the (award winning!) motivational speaker, author, fit, active running guy. I can still be all of those things, but I'm allowing myself to be vulnerable at times. It's ok to cry and be emotional. It's certainly fine to listen to advice and be told when it's time to slow down.

The journey is getting better. It's a more enjoyable ride. Writing this book has been a huge release and I hope that by sharing our story, we can help others reach out when they need to. Hope is out there whatever your situation. Do what works best for you but avoid sweeping it underneath the carpet and pretending it's not there. Find peace with yourself and reach out to those who love you.

In fact, as I write the final words of this book, Jules and I are sitting on cloud 9 at the moment. Only two days ago we won the Best Enterprising Business of the Year at the Northamptonshire SME Business Awards for the second year in a row.

The judges described our business, Future Toolbox, as people who are unique and passionate about what they do.

Someone said to us that it's amazing to be a finalist for an award and an incredible achievement to win it. To win two awards is just phenomenal! That fills both Jules and I with so much belief and inner confidence that, if we can achieve that, we can achieve anything.

I know that whatever this brain injury throws at me, I can be the person that I want to be and can own my life again.

A message for Jules:
Words can't express the love I have for my wonderful wife Jules. My absolute best friend and rock and the only person who will ever truly understand what we've been through. I've tried over and over again to apologise for the pain my brain injury has caused, but then have realised that we can do this together.

I wrote this inside our 16th wedding anniversary card (we don't normally do cards):

You're the best, and most wonderful person ever (and completely selfless too). I promise that life will keep getting better and it'll be fun and exciting. We'll get closer to carefree and full of adventure again. I love you more than ever.

A message to anyone who has suffered a brain injury:

I suppose I can say I'm a veteran of brain injuries now but I still don't fully understand them. In fact, I don't think anyone does. If you are suffering the effects, then reach out for support.

Also being in the business of personal development, keep working on yourself. Look for the positive things in life and enjoy them. Talk to happy, smiley people and remember those who love and care for you.

It's not your fault that you have a brain injury but it's not theirs either. You will get frustrated but so will they. Please don't lash out at those close to you. Explain how you are feeling and be honest with them. If it's too noisy, tell them you need to move somewhere quieter. If you're suffering fatigue, tell them you're suffering. And don't push yourself. Just listen to your body and listen to your mind. Finally, don't hide away. Keep pushing for help and support.

A message to anyone who loves someone who has suffered a brain injury:

For anyone who has a loved one suffering with brain injury, please try to stay calm. We don't understand what is going on at times and confronting or throwing logic at us probably won't always work. You will probably notice our symptoms before we do (lack of focus, concentration or confusion for example).

Empathy is a wonderful thing but saying, '*Oh yes, my memory is like that too, that's normal...*' doesn't help. These experiences are like nothing we've experienced before.

Every brain injury is different but one common theme is it will frustrate the person who has suffered the injury.

Here is something else I wrote to Jules recently and it sums up some good advice.

> When I'm sad, I need you to be happy.
> When I'm stressed, I need you to be calm.
> When I feel alone, I need a hug.
> When I'm confused, I need reassurance.
> When I'm anxious, I need relaxation.
> We will be strong forever.

(Is that a poem?)

Resources

Reference are provided for information purposes only and do not constitute endorsement of any websites or other sources. Readers should be aware that websites and links listed in this book may change.

Headway
www.headway.org.uk

Brain Injury Awareness UK
Group on Facebook

Mind
www.mind.org.uk

NHS
Severe Head Injury - www.nhs.uk/conditions/severe-head-injury
Community Brain Injury - www.nhft.nhs.uk/cbi (this is my local CBI group – check your local area for alternatives).

Mental Health First Aid England
www.mhfaengland.org

The Brain Charity
www.thebraincharitry.org.uk

Cassandra Farren (Writing to Release Trauma)
www.cassandrafarren.com

Future Toolbox
Jules and Mark's Personal Development Company
www.futuretoolbox.co.uk

From the Floor

Who is the best person to ask for advice? The answer, the person with experience.

Over the past year, I have been speaking to people living with brain injury on a daily basis. The best question to ask was, "Please share a top tip of how to cope with brain injury."

Here is a list of responses from brain injury sufferers, carers and people in support groups. I hope this helps.

Memory and Organisation

- I keep a log book/diary of things I've done or need to do.
- I write a shopping list on a whiteboard and ask everyone to add to it when they think of something, then take a photo on my phone.
- Same routine every morning, regardless.
- Post it notes help a lot.
- I have an Alexa reminds me to do everything.
- A pair of glasses in every room and I keep my keys on a long chain and fix it to my handbag so I don't go out without them.
- Try not to change a routine.
- Use alarms to help if you have a poor memory.
- I have a list in my notes app on my phone of my weekly/monthly bills so I know what to pay each week/month.
- Organise and label.
- Use a diary, post it notes round my home, and now use Alexa to remind me of stuff.
- Repeating something over and over to remember it.
- Take photos on phone of anything important, appointment letters, timetables/meetings etc.
- Use a phone diary for everything and remember to put your phone on.

- If I think of something I will need when I go shopping, I record it on my phone and then compile a written list later.
- Plan your weeks and write down a weekly plan with approximate times. Just realise that your batteries might run out faster. Rest when you need to. Don't be afraid to ask for help. If you're having a bad day you can usually put off a lot of things till the next day. Set alarms. Try and get up at the same time every day. Be kind to yourself.
- I have a variety of shopping bags scattered around the house for if ever I need to take something upstairs or carry something downstairs.

Communication

- If there is something important you need to say, write it down and keep your mouth zipped.
- Don't correct if you know what someone is trying to say, it can cause frustration and upset.
- Communication can work differently every day.
- Rest when you need rest. It's OK when you're not OK. But talk about it.

Positive Thinking

- Keep positive! Always aim for more.
- Never give up.
- Remember, you survived.
- Be yourself.
- Every little step is a humongous step for a person after brain injury.
- Never give up on yourself and love yourself.

Mental Wellbeing and Acceptance

- Be patient, the brain is slower at processing information.
- It is not always easy to understand but try to be accepting of the changes occurred from brain injury.
- Don't overwhelm yourself, confusion is likely to happen if you do.

- Be kind to yourself and take things one day at a time.
- Make yourself happy.
- Realising that some weeks I won't achieve my goal and that's fine.
- Take each day as it comes.
- Don't get mad, even if you have to repeat things...over & over & over.
- Just stop and let yourself catch up with yourself. For however long you need.
- Try the off switch.
- Don't smoke or drink.
- Take each day as it comes. Plan ahead for events you know you aren't going to be comfortable with such as family parties. Sleep when your body tells you to.
- At the start, don't panic, it will settle down. Don't compare old life to new life. Learn to manage your issues. Laugh when things go wrong and they will. Getting angry just makes things worse and you feel crap. Own your brain injury don't let it own you. Accept help when offered and get a support team in place. Finally enjoy yourself, it is what it is and fighting it is exhausting and a waste of energy.
- Sleep when you need to, over achieve when you can, grow into the new you slowly and if you find something that makes you happy, smile do it and feel free.
- As long as the person with brain injury is happy and healthy, it is OK.
- Never feel like it doesn't matter how you feel. It does matter.
- I think the most important thing is to allow yourself to sleep. After that go with it and don't try to fight it. Accept the new you and don't try to be as you were before.
- Neuro acupuncture and sleep.

Support

- Get someone near to you on board to help you with the things you find difficult. I needed help with some things like taking tablets, supervising cooking, feeding pets and picking the kids up. You need an understanding family member or partner if possible/available to discuss key activities with and help keep an eye out for potential pitfalls.

- A good support network, it really helps to talk.
- Be patient and be supportive of the person with the brain injury.
- As a carer don't argue when the issue is quite meaningless just change the subject.
- If you're a carer of someone with a brain injury saying things like "just do it, it's easy" or "come on I've explained it once." Things might need explaining 20 times for me to get it. I read a while ago a normal person's brain is capable of 12 hours work and a someone with a brain injury might just about get 4 hours brain power a day.
- To the carer - don't lose patience, just keep explaining things to me.
- Carer: it's ok to let things go. Confused days can really be hard for the person with brain injury. Be patient. However, take time to do things for yourself. Being there for someone is a good thing. Having someone outside the situation to talk to is a good idea.
- Brain injury is different for everyone. Take the time to sit down and explain things as many times as the person may need.
- Quite often it's the carer/family of someone with brain injury that needs to be educated as the changes in their loved one can be very hard to take in and come to terms with; believe me this comes from personal experience.
- One thing we should all remember is that we're all different and our injuries are more than likely different so we might need to sort things to suit our needs and capabilities and that we should always set aside me time.

Please remember, these are opinions of others and not necessarily ones we have tried and tested ourselves. They are tips from individuals in the general public and are not qualified professionals. Brain injury and the after effects of trauma aren't a one size fits all solution. Pick which could work for you but if you're really unsure, seek the help of professionals.

Printed in Great Britain
by Amazon